Sage ACT! 2011 Dashboard and Report Cookbook

Over 65 simple and incredibly effective recipes for creating and customizing exciting Dashboards and Reports from your ACT! data

Karen Fredricks

Roy Laudenslager

BIRMINGHAM - MUMBAI

Sage ACT! 2011 Dashboard and Report Cookbook

First published: February 2011

Production Reference: 1110211

Published by Packt Publishing Ltd.
32 Lincoln Road
Olton
Birmingham, B27 6PA, UK.

ISBN 978-1-849681-92-6

www.packtpub.com

Cover Image by David Guettirrez (bilbaorocker@yahoo.co.uk)

Credits

Authors
Karen Fredricks
Roy Laudenslager

Reviewers
Keith Wilson
Pat Egen

Acquisition Editor
Stephanie Moss

Development Editor
Hyacintha D'Souza

Technical Editor
Erika Fernandes

Indexer
Monica Ajmera Mehta

Editorial Team Leader
Vinodhan Nair

Project Team Leader
Lata Basantani

Project Coordinator
Vishal Bodwani

Proofreader
Aaron Nash

Production Coordinator
Shantanu Zagade

Cover Work
Shantanu Zagade

About the Authors

Karen Fredricks began her life rather non-technically growing up in Kenya. She likes to say that she developed her sense of humor while dodging bombs in Beirut where she attended high school. She graduated from the University of Florida and holds degrees in English, Theatre, and Accounting. She settled in Boca Raton where she includes tennis, trips to the gym, and cheering for the Gators in her busy schedule.

A true CRM expert, she is the author of over 10 **For Dummy** books, including titles on ACT!, SugarCRM, Outlook, Business Contact Manager, Office Live, and Marketing with Microsoft Office 2007. This is her sixth book devoted to ACT!.

Her firm, Tech Benders, customizes popular contact management and CRM software to help businesses grow by being more productive, efficient, and profitable. Karen believes in working smarter in order to have the time to enjoy life and tries to install that philosophy in her clients.

She is thrilled to being working with Roy Laudenslager as the co-author of this book. He has provided his expertise to several of her previous books and his knowledge of the ACT! Report Writer is second to none.

It may not take a villager to write a book, but it does take a number of helpful people! I'd like to thank Stephanie Moss, my Acquisition Editor, who saw the need for an ACT! title on Reports and Dashboards. Hyacintha D'Souza had the task of making sure my writing would be easily understood by readers. Vishal Bodwani took care of the scheduling of the book. This is my first Packt book and they provided guidance in every step of the way.

Gary Kahn was always there to support me, offer an occasional back rub, and provide diversions to help keep me on track.

And to my daughters, Andrea and Alyssa: I love you both!

Roy Laudenslager has spent his entire career working on computers. He likes to say he barely missed the vacuum tube computers. He has repaired them, written numerous training manuals about them, and spent many years troubleshooting them. He began working for Symantec when they combined all their technical support in a new site in Eugene, Oregon. When they acquired the ACT! program, he was one of the first ACT! support agents. He was already familiar with the ACT! program having used the DOS version at another company. He spent the next 10 years, supporting the ACT! program for Symantec, then InterACT Commerce Corporation, and finally for Sage Software. By the time he left, he was the lead support agent for ACT! *escalations*. Escalations are the problems that the regular support agents are unable to solve; his job was to solve the *unsolvable*. He also trained new support staff on database field modifications, reports, and synchronization. His expertise in the area of synchronization lead to the Knowledge Base document that he wrote for setting up synchronization, making it possible to synchronize ACT! 3 through 6 reliably. After 10 years in ACT! technical support, he wanted to become an ACT! Consultant so he left Sage and joined Karen Fredricks as part of Tech Benders to allow him to do what he loved to do: work with ACT! users!

He has worked with the ACT! reports since ACT! for Windows 2.0 and is known around Sage as the ACT! report writer guru. He wrote the 12 new reports that first appeared in ACT! 2010/12.

In the early part of his career, he spent several years working as a technical writer and authored many training and reference manuals.

While working in technical support for Symantec and later Sage, he contributed one or more articles monthly to the Easy ACT! newsletter. This body of work took place over a seven-year period and represented over 100 articles.

Most recently he was the Technical Editor for the Dummy books on ACT! versions 7-11.

I want to thank Karen Fredricks for her invitation to participate in writing this book.

I also want to thank my contacts at Packt for the opportunity, the prodding to keep me working and for the editorial feedback.

About the Reviewer

Keith Wilson is a recognized worldwide ACT! expert with over 18 years of experience. Working with a variety of different businesses ranging from very small organizations right up to large corporations, his knowledge of the product and his insights into how to get the very best from the product are second to none.

Through Keith's own endeavors, his previous employer Balanced Solutions quickly became one of the most respected Sage ACT! Business Partners in the UK and implemented the software in over 250 companies.

I would like to take this opportunity to personally thank my father for giving me a great grounding for the 18 years I worked for him and the opportunities that he has given me, both from a business perspective and also a personal one. Without his continued support, none of these achievements would have ever been fulfilled or appreciated.

For that Dad, I thank you and I love you very much.

---

www.PacktPub.com

Support files, eBooks, discount offers and more

You might want to visit www.PacktPub.com for support files and downloads related to your book.

Did you know that Packt offers eBook versions of every book published, with PDF and ePub files available? You can upgrade to the eBook version at www.PacktPub.com and as a print book customer, you are entitled to a discount on the eBook copy. Get in touch with us at service@packtpub.com for more details.

At www.PacktPub.com, you can also read a collection of free technical articles, sign up for a range of free newsletters and receive exclusive discounts and offers on Packt books and eBooks.

http://PacktLib.PacktPub.com

Do you need instant solutions to your IT questions? PacktLib is Packt's online digital book library. Here, you can access, read and search across Packt's entire library of books.

Why Subscribe?

- Fully searchable across every book published by Packt
- Copy and paste, print and bookmark content
- On demand and accessible via web browser

Free Access for Packt account holders

If you have an account with Packt at www.PacktPub.com, you can use this to access PacktLib today and view nine entirely free books. Simply use your login credentials for immediate access.

Instant Updates on New Packt Books

Get notified! Find out when new books are published by following *@PacktEnterprise* on Twitter, or the *Packt Enterprise* Facebook page.

This book is dedicated to both the new ACT! user who wants to learn about ACT! as quickly as possible and existing ACT! users who want to learn to take ACT! to the next level."

—Karen Fredricks

This book is dedicated to my wife Suzann for 44-years of wonderful partnership. This book would not have been possible without your love and understanding. Thank you from the bottom of my heart.

—Roy Laudenslager

Table of Contents

Preface

ACT! is the best-selling contact manager software in the market today. ACT! 2011 includes a variety of new Dashboards and reports that allow you to easily view important information about your business and your sales force. This cookbook is full of practical and immediately applicable recipes that will take you from being an ACT! Report and Dashboard novice to a report-writing pro in no time. The recipes will show you how to utilize the existing reports and Dashboards. You will also learn to use ACT!'s Report Writer and the Dashboard Designer so that you will be able to modify the existing report and Dashboard templates or create new ones, based on your own specifications.

The recipes begin by covering the most basic elements of the ACT! Reports and continue to include several recipes that will guide you through creating brand-new reports. If you have an ACT! database, you need to be able to access your information quickly and logically; this book will help you do just that.

What this book covers

Chapter 1, Exploring the ACT! Reports, serves as the most basic introduction to the ACT! reports. You'll become familiar with where to access reports and learn about the existing ACT! Reports.

Chapter 2, Filtering Data in Reports, covers the various filtering options available for the ACT! reports. You'll become familiar with the filtering options available prior to running a report along with the filter options within the actual report template.

Chapter 3, Creating a Quick Report, shows how to run the various quick reports available in the ACT! program. You'll be shown how to set up, control headers and footers, and run the various quick reports.

Chapter 4, Working with the Report Editor, introduces you to the structure, tools, and best practices for creating a basic report template. You will become familiar with using the properties tools to control the content and appearance of the report.

Chapter 5, Subreports and Scripting Techniques, continues showing you how to design a report. Here you move to the more advance techniques of report design working with custom sections and script programming.

Chapter 6, Labels and Envelopes, covers labels and envelopes which are specialized forms of the ACT! Reports. You'll be shown how to customize the standard label and envelope templates and how to design templates for custom sizes of both, labels and templates.

Chapter 7, Working with the ACT! Dashboards, serves as the most basic introduction to the ACT! Dashboard components. You'll become familiar with how to access the Dashboards, how to print them, and how to copy them into other documents.

Chapter 8, Filtering Dashboards, shows you how to filter the information that you see in the Contact, Activity, Opportunity, and Administrative Dashboard components.

Chapter 9, Editing Existing Dashboards, explains how to permanently change the various aspects of a Dashboard component including the display type, headers and footers, legends, totals, scales, and limits.

Chapter 10, Working with the Dashboard Designer, explains how to create a brand new Dashboard. You'll learn how to add and remove columns and rows to a Dashboard, add components, and custom data charts to a Dashboard and rearrange the dashboard components.

What you need for this book

You need to have ACT! versions 2009, 2010, or 2011 installed on your computer. And, although you can work with the demo database that automatically installs on your computer when you install ACT!, you'll have the best results if you work with your own database.

The chapters on reports use the demo database for all the screenshots.

Who this book is for

If you are an ACT! end-user who wants to learn about the existing reports and Dashboards available in ACT! 2009, 2010 and 2011, then this book is for you. If you are an ACT! administrator who wants to make changes to ACT!'s Dashboard and reporting features, you will also find this book helpful. No prior ACT! knowledge is necessarily required; however you'll find it helpful to have a good working knowledge of how to add data into ACT!, or to work with an ACT! database that has already been populated with data.

Conventions

In this book, you will find a number of styles of text that distinguish between different kinds of information. Here are some examples of these styles, and an explanation of their meaning.

Code words in text are shown as follows: "From the **Save As** window that opens you can choose to save the report in Adobe (`.pdf`), Rich-Text (`.rtf`), HTML (`.html`) or Text (`.txt`) file format".

New terms and **important words** are shown in bold. Words that you see on the screen, in menus or dialog boxes for example, appear in the text like this: "Click **OK** to run the report".

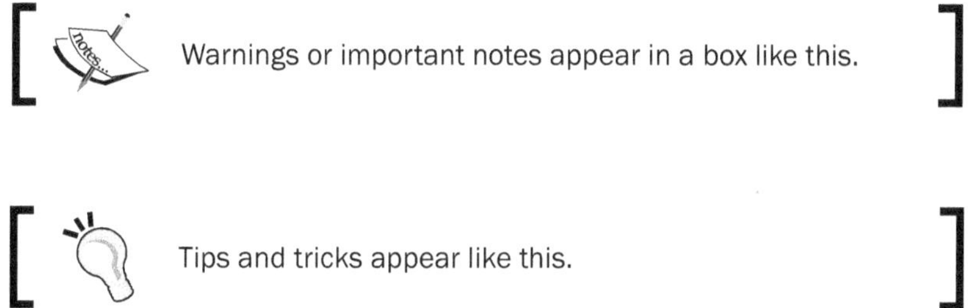

[Warnings or important notes appear in a box like this.]

[Tips and tricks appear like this.]

Reader feedback

Feedback from our readers is always welcome. Let us know what you think about this book—what you liked or may have disliked. Reader feedback is important for us to develop titles that you really get the most out of.

To send us general feedback, simply send an e-mail to `feedback@packtpub.com`, and mention the book title via the subject of your message.

If there is a book that you need and would like to see us publish, please send us a note in the **SUGGEST A TITLE** form on `www.packtpub.com` or e-mail `suggest@packtpub.com`.

If there is a topic that you have expertise in and you are interested in either writing or contributing to a book, see our author guide on `www.packtpub.com/authors`.

Customer support

Now that you are the proud owner of a Packt book, we have a number of things to help you to get the most from your purchase.

Errata

Although we have taken every care to ensure the accuracy of our content, mistakes do happen. If you find a mistake in one of our books—maybe a mistake in the text or the code—we would be grateful if you would report this to us. By doing so, you can save other readers from frustration and help us improve subsequent versions of this book. If you find any errata, please report them by visiting `http://www.packtpub.com/support`, selecting your book, clicking on the errata submission form link, and entering the details of your errata. Once your errata are verified, your submission will be accepted and the errata will be uploaded on our website, or added to any list of existing errata, under the Errata section of that title. Any existing errata can be viewed by selecting your title from `http://www.packtpub.com/support`.

Piracy

Piracy of copyright material on the Internet is an ongoing problem across all media. At Packt, we take the protection of our copyright and licenses very seriously. If you come across any illegal copies of our works, in any form, on the Internet, please provide us with the location address or website name immediately so that we can pursue a remedy.

Please contact us at `copyright@packtpub.com` with a link to the suspected pirated material.

We appreciate your help in protecting our authors, and our ability to bring you valuable content.

Questions

You can contact us at `questions@packtpub.com` if you are having a problem with any aspect of the book, and we will do our best to address it.

1 Exploring the ACT! Reports

In this chapter, we will cover:

- Using the ACT! Reports menu
- Working with the Reports view
- Adding reports to the Favorites List
- Removing a Report from the Favorites List
- Running a Report from the Favorites List
- Choosing a Report Output Option
- Finding the Default Location of the ACT! Reports

Introduction

Once you've added information into ACT! the next step is to be able to view that information in an organized fashion. With over 60 reports to choose from, you'll probably be able to find a report that will give you exactly the information you're looking for.

After reading this chapter, you'll be familiar with the various *out of the box* ACT! Reports. You'll even find where they are located on your computer. You'll learn how to find the reports you need and more importantly, how to organize them into favorites so that you'll be able to find them again. You'll also learn how to run a report, and find out how to share those reports with colleagues.

Using the ACT! Reports menu

The most common method of running a report is from the Reports menu, which is located on any of the **ACT! views**. Ironically, you'll even find the Reports on the menu bar in the Reports view, which we will be covering later in this chapter.

Getting ready

Some of you may have used other software programs that allow you to filter a report after you run it. For example, your accounting software might let you run a Profit and Loss statement, and then change the date range once the report is run.

ACT! works a bit differently. The ACT! Reports offer only very basic filtering options; if a report doesn't contain the filter options you're looking for then you must do the filtering prior to running the report. For example, if you wanted to create a Phone List report of all of your customers, you'd first need to **Create a Lookup** or run a query for the customers in your database.

How to do it...

Follow these steps to run a report:

1. Create a **Lookup of Contact**, **Company**, or **Group** records that you wish to include in your report.
2. Click on **Reports** in the menu bar, and then click the report name that you wish to run. The **Define Filters** dialog box appears as seen in the following screenshot:

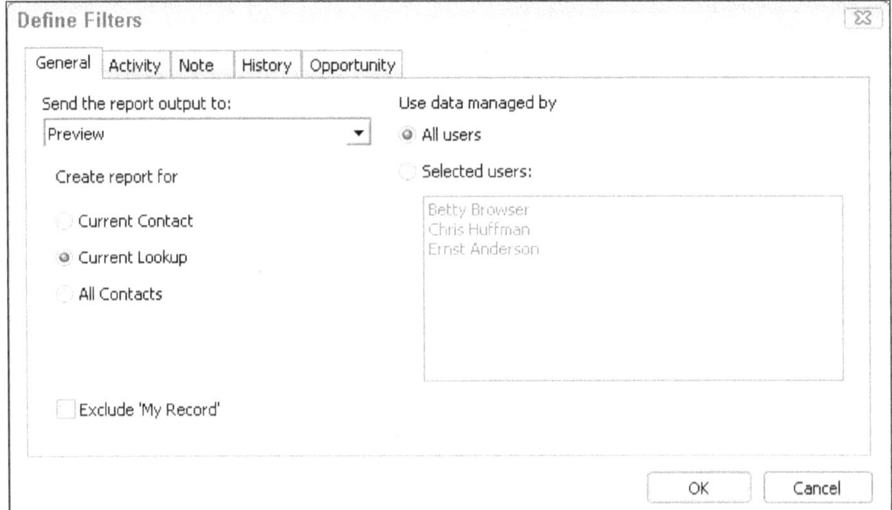

3. Verify that the report filters are correct. You'll be learning more about the various filter options in the next chapter.
4. Click **OK** to run the report.

How it works...

The Reports menu includes a main area of contact reports, as well as sub-areas for Group, Company, and Opportunity Reports. While this organization seems like a good idea on paper, in reality over half of the ACT! Reports are not listed on the ACT! Reports menu.

There's more...

As we mentioned earlier, there are over 60 reports that come with *ACT! out of the box*. However, because the Reports menu is a carry-over from a much older version of ACT!, you'll find fewer than 30 of the ACT! Reports actually listed in the Reports menus. And, to make finding a report even more difficult, ACT!'s file structure places all of the reports in a single folder rather than organizing the reports into more logical sub-folders.

If the report you wish to run is not listed under the **Reports** menu, click **Group Reports**, **Company Reports**, or **Opportunity Reports** to see more choices. And if you still can't find the report you'd like then click **Other Contact Reports...** to see all of the ACT! Reports.

Learning a bit more about specific reports

It may be helpful to have an idea about the information that appears in a few of the ACT! Reports.

- The first three reports listed in the **Reports** menu (the **Contact Report**, **Contact Directory**, and **Phone List**) will provide you with a full page, paragraph, or a single line of information about your current Lookup of contacts
- The **History Summary** reports give you a physical count of the various cleared history items
- The **Source of Referrals** report is based on information that you've inputted into the Referred by field

A warning about the "Other" Report menu options

You'll see 10 Contact reports listed on the top half of the reports menu. These reports are all based on the generic contact ACT! fields that come with a basic ACT! database. You'll also notice an option for **Other Contact Reports...** at the bottom of this list. Unfortunately, clicking this option will result in the **Select Report** dialog box you see in the following screenshot, which shows you not just **additional** contact reports but it also **all** of the ACT! Reports:

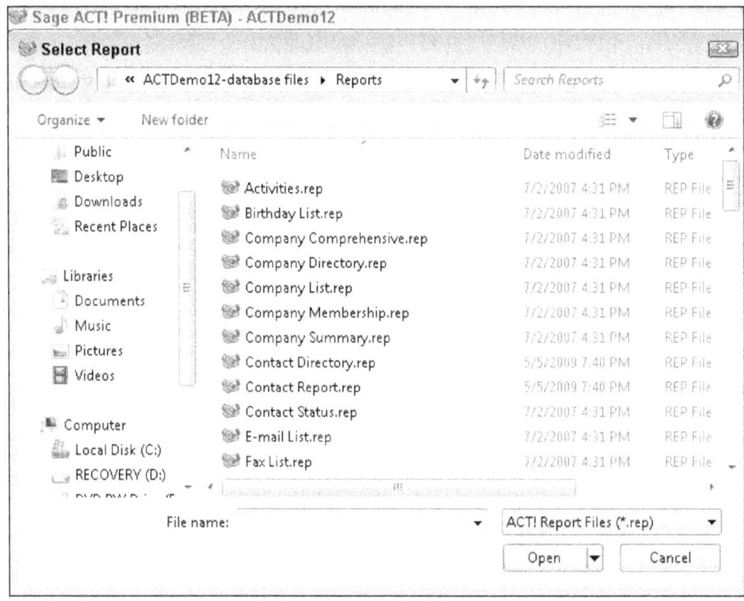

In addition to showing you additional Contact ACT! Reports, it also shows you additional Group, Company, and Opportunity Reports as well.

If you navigate from the basic reports menu to the Group, Company, or Opportunity reports sub-menus, you'll notice that they all contain an *other* section like the one you see in the following screenshot:

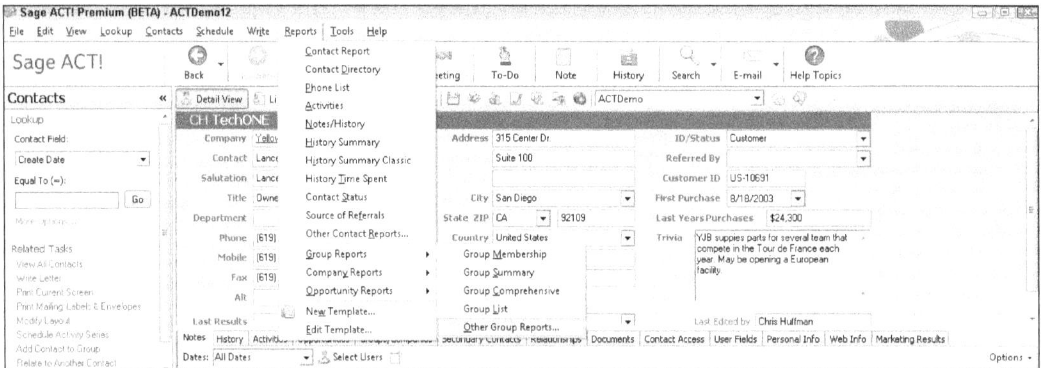

You probably expect that if you click the **Other Group Reports...** option you'll be transported to a listing of various other Group reports not included in the Reports menu. Unfortunately, you're taken back to the **Select Report** dialog box shown earlier that lists **all** of the ACT! Reports.

It might seem to be a logical assumption that if you are in the Groups view and click on **Reports** in the *menu bar*, you'll see a list of all the Group reports, and that if you are in the Company view you can click on **Reports**, and *you'll* be treated to a list of Company reports. However, the Report menu is exactly the same in every one of the ACT! views.

See also

Because the Reports menu only scratches the surface of the entirety of the reports included with ACT!, you'll probably find yourself using the Reports view more often.

[ Make sure to read the section, *Working with the Reports View* later in this chapter.]

Using the Reports view

Up until ACT! 2010/12, the only way that you could run a report was through the Report menu. However, as more reports were added to the ACT! program, no changes were made to the Reports menu. It soon became apparent that the reports area needed somewhat of a facelift and so the **Reports** view entered the picture. The Reports view solved a few critical reporting issues:

- You could see a full listing of all the ACT! Reports
- You could designate any of the reports as favorites so that you could find them again easily in the future
- You could add a description to a report to help identify it again in the future
- You could delete and/or edit any of the ACT! Reports

Getting ready

It's nice to keep things organized, especially when you are working with over 60 reports. By using the Reports view you will be assured that you will be able to find exactly the report you want. You can also think of the Reports view as a *one-stop shop* for all your Reporting needs.

The Reports view will allow you to:

- Run reports
- Edit reports
- Edit report properties
- Delete reports
- Organize the reports into your favorites

How to do it...

1. Navigate to the ACT! Reports view using one of the following methods:
    - Click **View** on any of the ACT! menu bars and then choose **Reports**
    - Click **Reports** from the nav bar that runs along the left-hand side of any ACT! window

    The **Reports** view will appear like the one you see in the following screenshot:

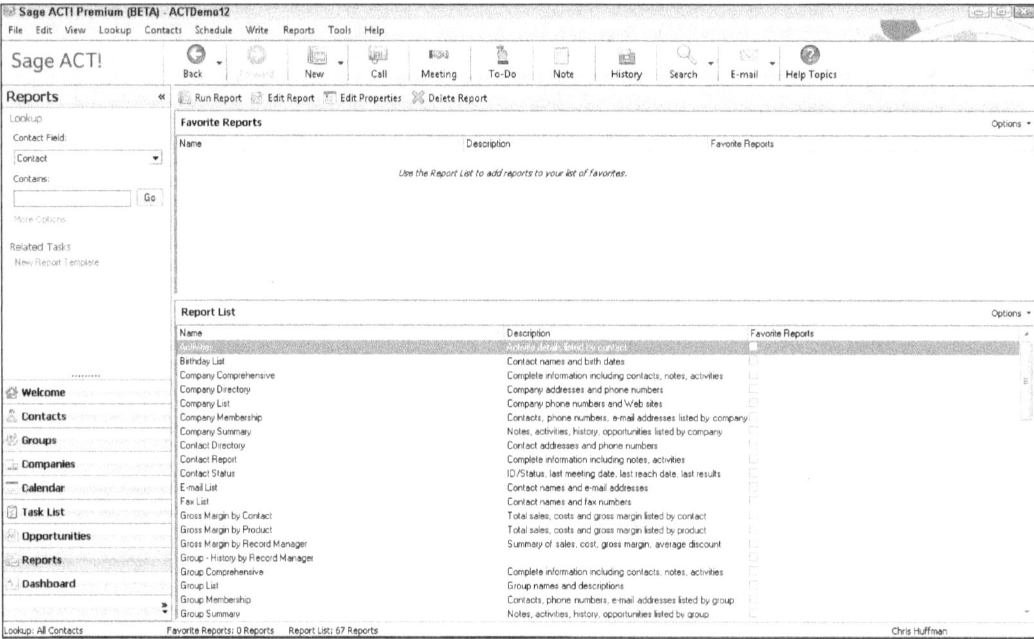

    You will notice that it is split into two windows: **Favorite Reports** and the **Report List**.

2. Select a report from the **Report List** by clicking on it once.
3. At this stage you can select one of the buttons on the **Reports** view toolbar to **Run Report**, **Edit Report**, and **Delete Report** for an existing report.

How it works...

The **Favorite Reports** area on the top of the screen shows a list of the reports that you have defined as your **Favorite Reports**, and the **Report List** on the bottom half of the screen lists every one of the ACT! Reports. As you modify one of the reports listed on the **Report List**, the corresponding item will update on the **Favorite Reports** area as well.

You will also notice that a status bar runs along the bottom of the **Reports** view. The status bar will give you a running total of the number of reports you have designated as *Favorites* as well as the total number of reports that are attached to the current database.

There's more...

We will be discussing running reports, editing their properties, and deleting reports in more detail later in this chapter.

The default order of the Report List

You will notice that the reports are listed in alphabetical order which means that the Group reports (at least those that begin with the word *Group*) appear together in the list, and the Opportunity reports beginning with the word *Opportunity* appear together.

Adding the modification date to the Report List

You can actually make one slight modification to the Report view. You'll notice the **Options** button that appears in the top-right corner of both the **Favorite Reports** and **Report List** areas. Give it a click and chose **Customize Columns...**—this happens to be your **only** choice. Select **Last Modified** from the **Available fields** area and then click the double-pointing right-arrows(**>>**) to move it to the **Show as columns in this order** area on the right.

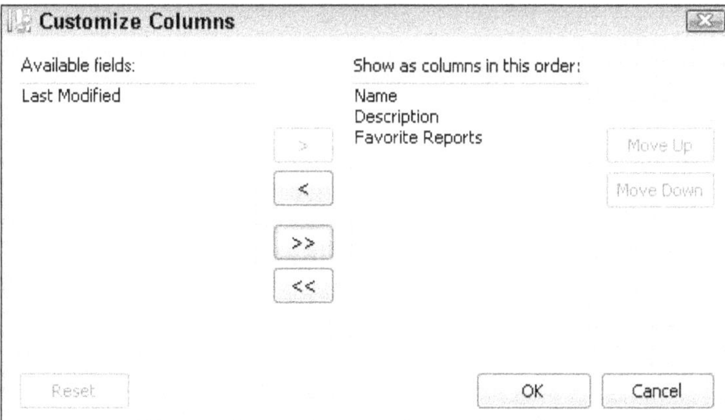

Once added, you can click on the **Last Modified** column head to sort your reports chronologically by the date on which they were last modified so that you'll be able to easily identify any of the reports that you've created and/or modified.

Just in case you are chomping at the bit to start editing a report or two, you can read the next few chapters in this book where we'll show you how to do just that.

Running a report from the Report view

Entering information into your database is the hard part. The easy part comes from running a report so that you can better analyze that data.

Getting ready

The only thing you'll want to do before heading for the Reports view is to create a Lookup of contacts specific to your reports. For example, if you want to run the **Source of Referrals** report to find out how all your top customers found out about you in the first place, you'll want to create a **Lookup for Top Customers**.

How to do it...

1. Navigate to the ACT! Reports view.
2. Select the report you wish to run from either the **Favorite Reports** or **Report List**.
3. Click the **Run Report** button on the **Report view** toolbar. Alternatively you can double-click the name of the report you want to run. Depending on the report you choose, you'll see a **Define Filters** dialog box similar to the one shown previously.
4. Click **OK** to run the report.
5. Click the red **X** to close the report when you're finished viewing it.

How it works...

The ACT! Report will include only those contacts that are included as part of your current lookup. In addition, as you run a report you can filter the contents of that report. For example, you might create a lookup of all of your customers, and then filter your report to include only notes that you've added about those customers in the last 30 days.

There's more...

You can learn about the various filtering options in the next chapter. You can permanently alter the filtering options in a report from the Report Designer, which we'll discuss later in this book. For example, you may always want to run one of the Opportunity reports for the prior month, or save your pipeline as a PDF file.

Limiting access to Report Data

Rightfully so, many ACT! users worry about the security of their data. As a business owner you might be concerned that one of your ACT! users could run a report and then *run off with* your data. All of the ACT! Reports are automatically added to the database and appear in the Report view. Any users who can access the database can run the report. However, if you are using ACT! Premium and have limited the access rights at the contact level, those access rights *cascade* down to the report level.

For example, you may be worried that one of your sales people could run the Contact Report and consequently have a nice listing of all of your customers. However, if you have limited the access to those customers so that your sales person can't access them, the sales person can still run the report, but it will not contain any of the contacts to which he has no access.

Choosing a Report Output Option

Once you've found a report that provides you with the information you need, you are ready to run with it. As usual, ACT! is up to the challenge and provides you with a number of options in which to view your report.

Getting ready

As you have already learned, the procedure for running a report generally starts by creating a Lookup of the contacts that you want to include in the report, followed by a trip to the Reports view.

How to do it...

1. Select the report that you want to run from the Report view.
2. Click on the **Run Report** button. The **Define Filters** dialog window will open.
3. Click the **Send the report output to:** drop-down arrow.

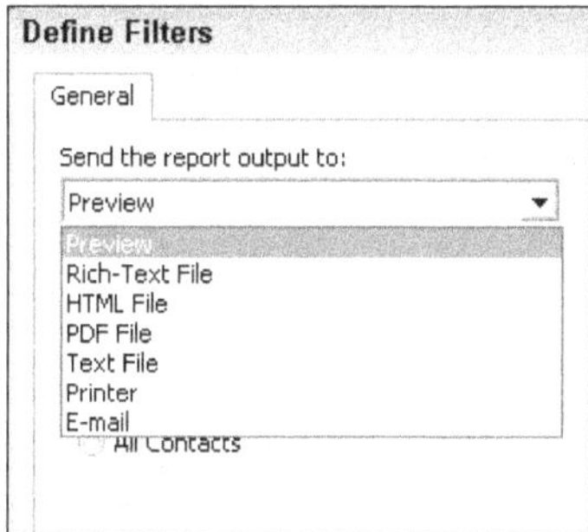

4. By default, the **Send the report output to:** field is set to **Preview.** This is a good option because it allows you to view the report, and optionally print the report as well from the **Print Preview** window.

5. Click **OK** to run the report. The **Print Preview** window will open like the one you see in the following screenshot:

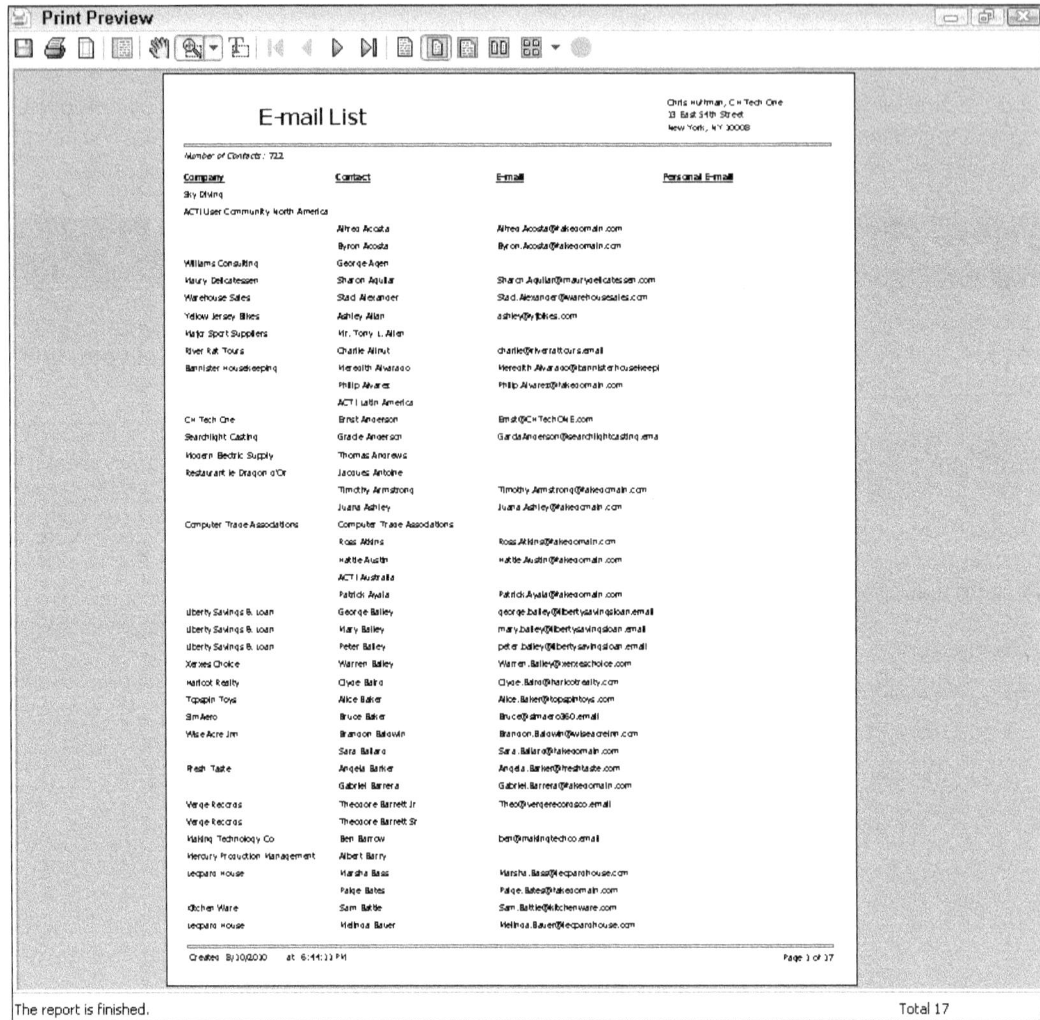

6. The **Print Preview** comes equipped with a nice selection of tools. As you hover your cursor over each one of them, a tooltip will magically appear telling you what the button does.

7. Maximize the **Print Preview** window and select the zoom-in tool (the small magnifying glass) on the toolbar to zoom in on a section of the report you would like to see a bit more clearly. Unfortunately the **Print Preview** window can be a little small for most of our eyes!
8. Click the right-pointing arrow in the **Print Preview** window to move to the next page in the report, or the **Last Page** icon to view the last page of the report which often contains report totals.
9. When you are ready to print the report, click the *Printer* icon.
10. Click the *red* **X** to close the **Print Preview** window.

How it works...

In order to preview a report you must have Adobe Acrobat reader installed on your computer. Fortunately, it's included on the ACT! installation disk and installs automatically as part of the ACT! installation.

There's more...

Once you've run the report, and optionally printed it, the Print Preview window remains open. At this point you can close the Preview window and run the report again selecting a different output option.

If you are really happy with the report, you can click the *File Save icon* in the top left corner of the **Print Preview** window to save the report. From the **Save As** window that opens you can choose to save the report in Adobe (`.pdf`), Rich-Text (`.rtf`), HTML (`.html`) or Text (`.txt`) file format.

Saving a report as a PDF is a great idea if you want to permanently preserve the data in a report. If you don't save the report, the report might look a bit different if your data has changed since the previous run.

In addition to the Preview option, there are six other output options. Five of them can also be run from the **Print Preview** window. The sixth one, e-mail, is a really helpful feature. When you choose this option a new e-mail message will appear—with a copy of your report already attached!

Editing Reports in the Reports view

It's nice to keep things organized, especially when you're working with over 60 reports. By tweaking the Reports view, you will be insured that you will be able to find exactly the report you want.

Getting ready

Before you go about changing the Reports view, it's a good idea to familiarize yourself with the various reports so that you know which ones will work for you. When you install ACT! a demo database installs as well that is populated with lots of data. You might want to open the demo database and preview any of the reports that sound appealing. Once you have had a chance to view them, jot down a list of your favorites.

How to do it...

1. Navigate to the ACT! Reports view. Select a report from the **Report List** by clicking on it once.
2. Click on the **Edit Properties** button. The **Edit Properties** dialog box will open like the following screenshot:

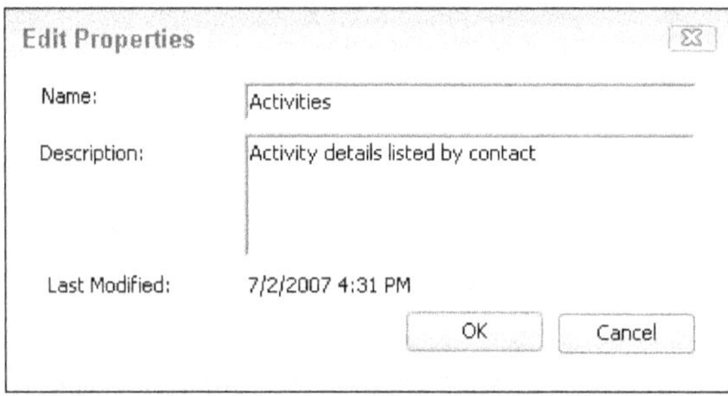

3. Enter a new name for a report in the **Name** field that will make it easier for you to identify in the future.
4. (Optional) Enter a new description for the report in the **Description** field.
5. Click **OK** to close the dialog box and save your changes.

How it works...

As you modify the properties of an item listed in the **Reports** view, the corresponding report will update as well if you had already added it to the Favorite Reports.

There's more...

The main reason for changing the report properties is to help you organize the reports in a way that makes sense to you. For example, many companies are used to using what they call a **Face Sheet** and may want to rename the **Contact Report** accordingly.

Changing the sort order in the Report view

The reports are listed in alphabetical order which means that the Group reports (at least those that begin with the word *Group*) appear together in the list and the Opportunity reports beginning with the word *Opportunity* appear together.

Wouldn't it be nice if all the reports appeared together according to their type? Well, they can. Simply tweak the description of each report slightly by adding *Contact* to the front of all the Contact reports, *Opportunity* in front of all the Opportunity reports, and so on. You can then sort the report list by Description by clicking the **Description column header** and have your reports neatly sorted by category.

Deleting a Report

There's another button lurking on the Reports View icon bar—the **Delete Report** button. If you delete a report it is permanently removed from the database which means that none of the other users will be able to access it. Deleting a report is **not** the same thing as removing a report from the Favorites list, which you will learn later in this chapter.

Rather than permanently deleting a report, consider renaming it by placing an *X* in front of it so that all the reports you don't need fall to the end of the Report List.

Keeping a list of Favorite reports

In the older versions of ACT!, it wasn't critically important to keep your reports well organized; it was easy enough to just navigate to the Reports menu, or find one of the handful of reports that had been left off of the Report menu. However, with a dozen new reports added to ACT! 2010, and another 10 added to ACT! 2011, it is now imperative that you organize the reports. After all, none of the new reports appear on the Reports menu. Further complicating the issue is the fact that so many of the reports have similar names.

Getting ready

In the previous section, we suggested that you jot down a list of the reports that seemed to be a good match for your reporting needs. This list will prove helpful when editing the **Favorite Reports** section of the **Reports** view.

How to do it...

1. From the navigation bar, click **Reports**. The **Reports** view will open.
2. Select the **Favorites Reports** checkbox next to any of the reports that you would like to run on a regular basis.

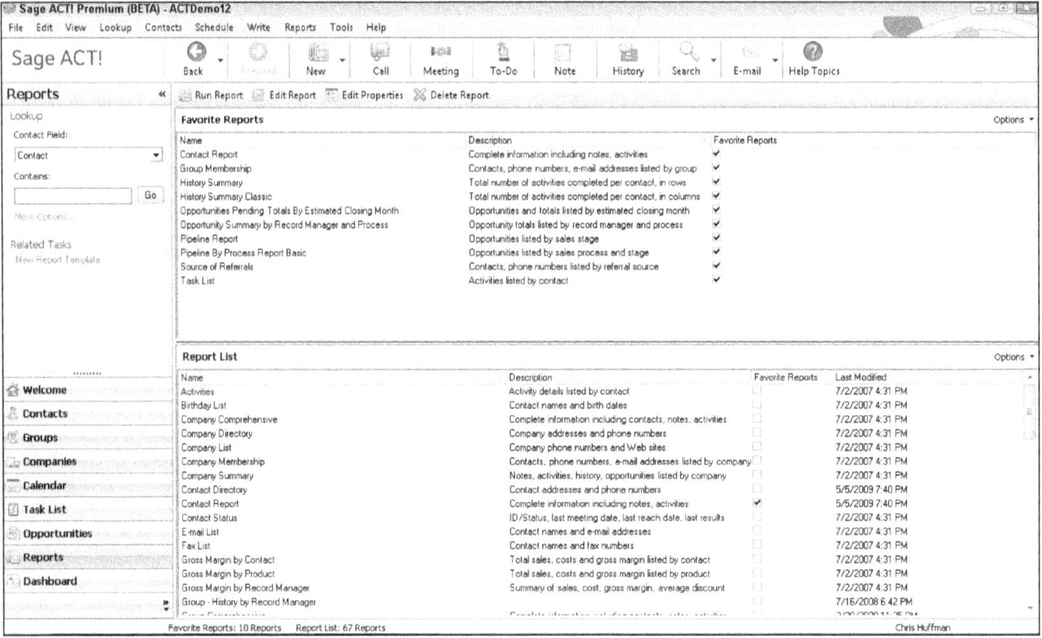

How it works...

Any of the reports that you selected from the **Reports List** will automatically appear in the **Favorite Reports** area.

There's more...

You can select as many reports as you want to become your favorites. And, if you edit the name or description of a report in either of the lists, the corresponding report will change in the other list as well. You can also sort the two lists differently if the mood strikes you.

Changing the size of the Report view area

As you add more and more reports to your Favorite Reports, you might want to increase the area that is devoted to that section. You can do this by hovering your mouse on the dividing line between the two sections of the Reports view, and dragging the line lower on the screen.

As I always say, easy come easy go. That philosophy holds true with the Favorite Reports as well. If you decide that a report just isn't as special as you originally thought, simply remove the checkmark and the report will disappear from your Favorite Reports.

Finding the default location of the ACT! Reports

Running an ACT! Report is easy because you're given a number of options for finding reports. You can run a report from the Report menu that appears in the menu bar of every ACT! view, or you can choose a report from the Report view. Either of these methods is actually a shortcut for running a report template located within the supplementary folders area of your database.

It's a good idea to know the exact location on your computer that stores the actual report templates. For example, you might need to move some of your reports to a new computer, or save a report that someone else developed for you.

How to do it...

1. Click ACT!'s **Help menu**, and then click **About ACT!**. The **About ACT!** dialog box appears.
2. Click the **Database Information** button. The **Database Information** dialog box appears.
3. Scroll down the list in the **Database Settings Information** section to the **Supplemental File Location** entry. The location of the reports will appear in the **Current Value** section.

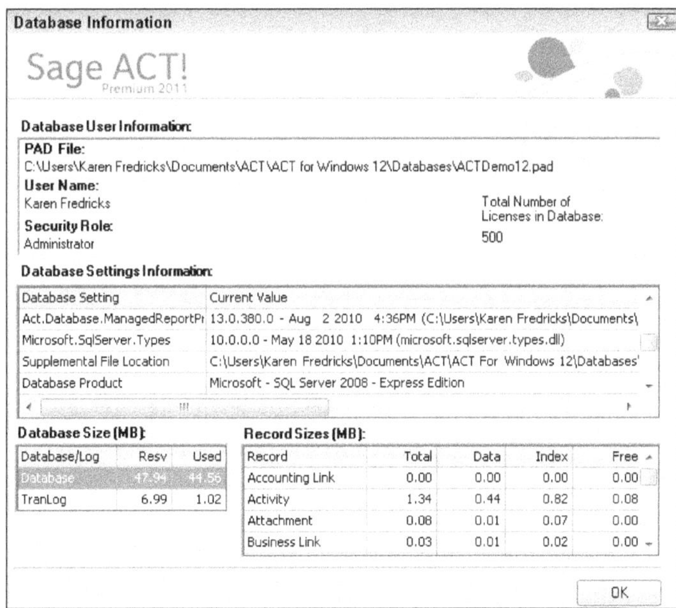

How it works...

When you create an ACT! database, a set of supplementary folders is created as well. These folders house the various files associated with your database such as your layouts, attachments, and reports.

There's more...

If the field structure of two databases is the same, you can share reports between the databases by copying the report files of one database and pasting them into the reports folder of the other database.

2

Filtering Data in Reports

In this chapter, we will cover:

- Filtering based on a contact field lookup
- Filtering Contact reports
- Filtering based on a contact activity lookup
- Filtering Notes and History in reports
- Filtering activities in reports
- Filtering Groups reports
- Filtering Company reports
- Filtering Opportunity reports
- Preset filters for most used option

Introduction

The ACT! database is very useful for storing data in an structured manner. As your database grows, you will likely want to extract and filter the data in an organized manner.

Reports provide a way to extract your data in an organized manner. However, a report that simply dumps all your data to a printer, no matter how well it is organized, would be of little use. You would still need to search through the printed copy to find just what you wanted. What you need is a means to focus the report on the data that you're interested in. The process used is called **filtering**.

The ACT! Reports provide a variety of filtering options; most are applied when you run the report, but some require that you take actions in the database before you run the report.

After reading this chapter, you will be able to use the report filtering to focus your report on the desired data.

Filtering based on a contact field lookup

The simplest form of filtering for a report is to limit the report to only a portion of the contacts in your database. That way you only print the records that meet specific criteria. This type of filtering is done prior to running the report, and as such isn't directly part of running the report, but it's necessary for the filtering process in the report itself.

Getting ready

Before you create the lookup, you need to decide which report you plan to run, because the lookup needs to relate to the report you're creating. You also need to decide the criteria for the lookup. The example we'll use is the **Contact Directory report** and the lookup will be based on City and State.

How to do it...

1. On the **Detail Contact** screen, right-click on the **State** field and choose **Lookup State**.
2. If you don't see the full dialog box, click on **Show more options**. Verify the field type and type of query (Starts With) and use the dropdown to select the desired **State**. Make sure the **For the current lookup** is **Replace Lookup**.

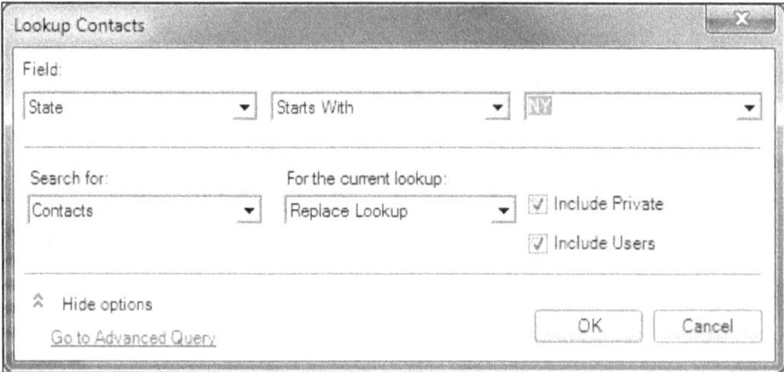

3. Click the **OK** button. The screen will switch to the List View with a list of all the contacts in New York state.
4. Click on **Detail View** to switch back.
5. Right-click on **City field** and choose **Lookup City**.

6. Verify the field and query type and use the dropdown to select the desired **City**. In the **For the current lookup** box, use the dropdown to choose **Narrow Lookup**.

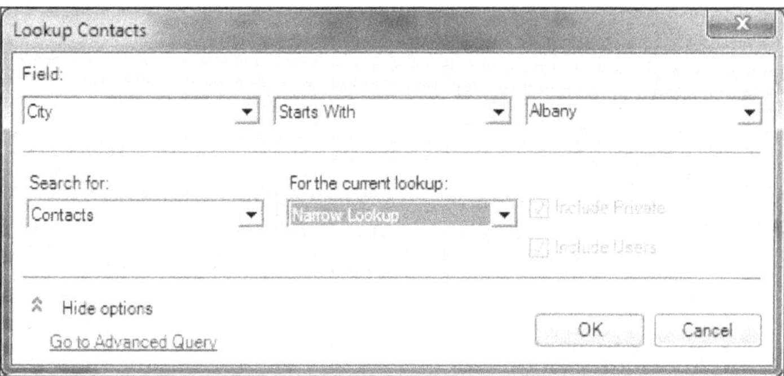

How it works...

This procedure is a simple query chain. The first lookup examines the entire database and creates a temporary list of all the contacts in the specified state. The second lookup, by specifying Narrow Lookup, causes the query to look only at the temporary list, not the whole database, and then creates a new temporary list of contacts who are in the specified city within the specified state. This lookup is retained by the ACT! program until ACT! is closed or another new lookup is performed. It is called the **Current Lookup** and can then be used to filter a report.

There's more...

What was used here was a simple query lookup. The ACT! program provides other methods of querying the database that are more complex. As a general rule, if you need to create a lookup that is based on a couple of field values, the method shown here is a good one to use. A more complex query is shown in a later procedure.

A special point to remember: the fields you use to create a lookup don't need to be used in the report you run. The lookup you create tells the report which contact to use, not the fields in the report.

Filtering Contact reports

We've created a lookup of contacts to include in the reports, so now we move to running a contact report. The lookup we created will be used to filter the contacts included in the report, and can be used with any of the contact based reports as well as the labels and envelopes. Here we will use the **Contact Directory** report.

How to do it...

1. From any screen in the ACT! program, click on **Reports** in the navigation bar on the left-hand side of the screen.
2. In the **Report List**, double-click on the **Contact Directory** report.
3. In the **Define Filters** dialog there are several filter and output options to select.

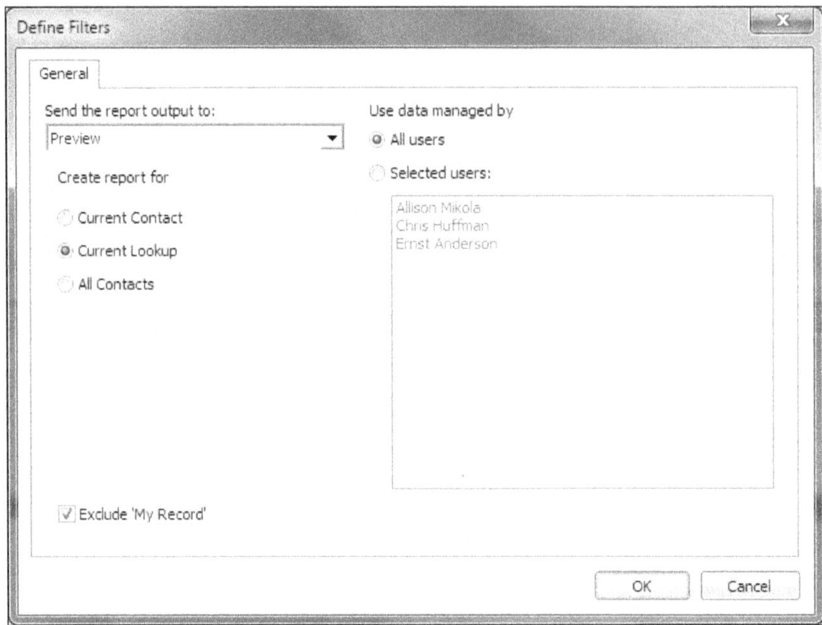

4. Click on the radio button for **Current Lookup** to use the lookup we created as a filter.
5. Make sure **Exclude 'My Record'** is checked.

In most cases, you will want to exclude the My Record because your report will be focused on contact data. In some cases, you may have pertinent data recorded on your My Record and in that case you would want to include the My Record.

6. Select all users in **Use data managed by** to include all the contacts in the lookup.
7. Select **Preview** for the output desired.
8. Click **OK** to run the report with these filter options.

How it works...

This is the main Define filters dialog that is used to run reports, labels, and envelopes. There will be changes to some of the options and additional tabs depending on the capabilities of the report you select. The **Create report for** section provides a selection of the records included in the report. Most reports give these three options or ones similar when you run the report. In some cases, if you haven't created an applicable lookup, the Current lookup option will not be available. In most cases you don't want to include information from the **My Record**, but the filter option is included for those cases when you *do* want to include the My Record. The **Use data managed by** filter allows you to select all users, a single user, or a combination of users.

There's More...

The **Create report for** filter has an additional capability, specifically for the Current lookup and the **All contacts** options. The **All contacts** option uses a default sort of company for a contact report. The **Current lookup** option uses the sort order of the lookup you have created. However, if the report template has a built in sort, that will override any pre-sort.

See also

Refer to Chapter 4, Working with the Report Editor, for more information on built in sorts.

Filtering based on a contact activity lookup

In the first task, we created a relatively simple lookup based on two contact fields. In this task we will create a more complex lookup based on contact activity. The resulting lookup can be used with any contact report. The contact activity lookup is very flexible with a number of options. For this task, we do a relatively simple lookup of any call activity recorded in history since a specified date.

How to do it...

1. Click on **Contacts** on the **navigation** bar on the left-hand side of the ACT! screen.
2. Click on the **Lookup** menu and select **Contact Activity...**.
3. In the **Contact Activity** dialog, click on the radio button next to **Changed**.
4. For **Since Date**, click on the dropdown and click on a date in the calendar displayed.
5. For **Search In**, uncheck **Contact fields**, **Notes**, **Opportunities**, and **Activities**.

6. Click on the **Histories** dropdown and click **None**.

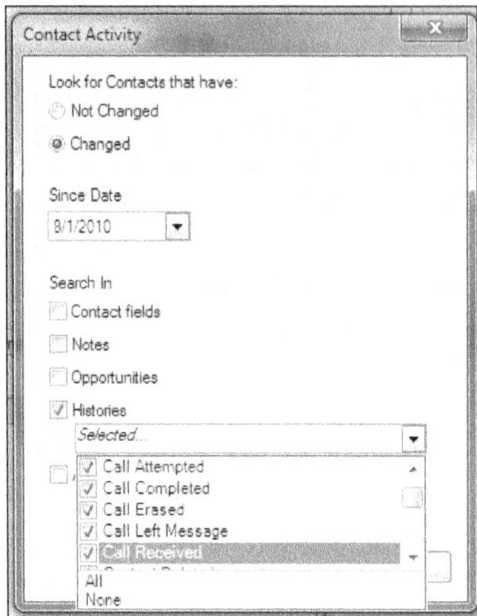

7. Scroll the list of history types to the call types and click on all five call types as shown in the preceding screenshot.
8. Press the *Tab* key to save the type selection.
9. Click **OK** to execute the query.

How it works...

In this case, we wanted to filter for those contacts that we had tried to call or we had a conversation within a time period ending at today. This query checks all the history records for two things:

- One of the specified call history types
- A last modified date within the date range selected

When a history record is found that meets the criteria, the contact record it's linked to is added to the lookup list. As in the first task, the temporary lookup list is retained and can be used for the **Current Lookup** option in the report filters.

There's more...

The contact activity lookup we created was very simple, but the contact activity lookups can be very complex. For example, we created our lookup based on records that were changed within the time period ending with today. This is very good for tracking what we *have* done. But a more powerful version where we want to plan future activity would be **Not Changed**. With this we can create a report that lists all the contacts that we had *not* called recently. Because it's somewhat hidden, this powerful lookup is often overlooked as a useful filter.

Filtering Notes and History in reports

In the previous task, we created a lookup using the contact's activity. While the resulting lookup can be used with any contact report, it's most often used for the Notes History report.

How to do it...

1. From any screen in the ACT! program, click on **Reports** in the navigation bar on the left-hand side of the screen.
2. In the **Report List**, double-click on the **Notes - Histories** report.
3. Click the radio button, next to **Current Lookup**.
4. Check **Exclude 'My Record'**.

In most cases, you will want to exclude the My Record because your report will be focused on contact data. In some cases, you may have pertinent data recorded on your My Record, and in that case you would want to include the My Record.

5. Click the dropdown for **Send the report output to** and select **Preview**.
6. Click the radio button for **All users**.

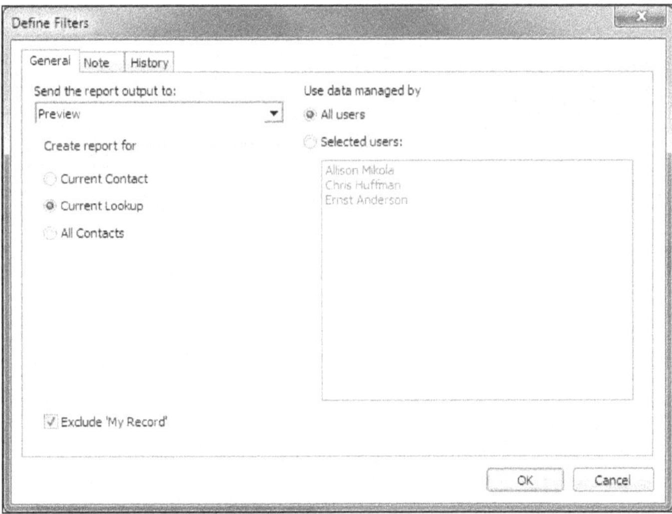

7. Click on the **Note** tab and follow these steps:
    i. Check **Notes**.
    ii. Click the radio button for **All users**.
    iii. Click the dropdown for **Date Range** and select **Last Month**.

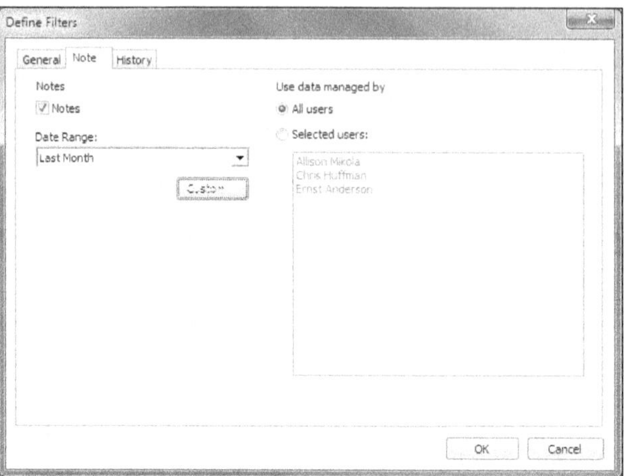

8. Click the **History** tab and perform the following steps:
    i. Check **History** and uncheck **E-mail** and **Attachments**.
    ii. Click the radio button for **All users**.
    iii. Click the dropdown for **Date range** and select **Last Month**.

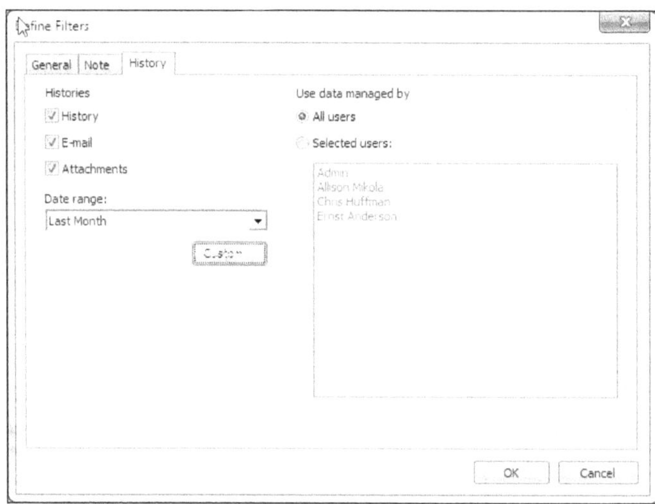

    iv. Click **OK** to run the report with these filter options.

How it works...

With the **Notes - Histories** report, the **Define Filters** dialog has two additional tabs. Besides the **General** tab there is a **Note** and a **History** tab. Each of these tabs provides additional filtering for the report. The **General** tab provides filter selections based on the contact record. This is the primary filtering for the report, because the filters here decide which contact record to include in the report. Because we selected the **Current Lookup** filter option, the report will be based on a lookup created prior to starting the report.

The contact Notes and Histories have a one-to-many relationship with the contact record, so there can be several note and history entries linked to the contact record. The Note and History tabs allow the setting of additional filters for those records. In the **Note** tab, there is a checkbox that, if unchecked, allows excluding all notes from the report. The **Date range** filter allows limiting the notes included to a specified date range. The dropdown provides several common date range options and the custom button opens a **start** and **end calendar** so that any date range you may need, can be specified. The **Use data managed by** filter allows you to select notes entered by all users, a single user or a combination of users.

The filters on the **History** tab are basically the same as on the **Notes** tab, except that you have checkboxes to include or exclude specific types or all types of histories. If either **Attachments** or **E-mail** are unchecked, the history types are additionally filtered to exclude history types such as **Field Change**.

There's more...

The filtering of users in this report and other reports where there are multiple filter tabs has a power that's not immediately obvious, but can throw your results off if not selected correctly. Every separate entry in the ACT! database such as the contact profile, a note entry, a history entry and so on; each of these individual records has a record manager, typically the user that actually makes the record entry.

When you select all users on the Contact tab, all the contacts in the lookup used for the report will be included. However, if you select a specific user, only those contact records where that user is the record manager will be included in the report, thus narrowing the lookup used for the report.

A similar thing happens with the user selections on the **Note** and **History** tabs, except now it's the record manager of each note or history (typically the user that entered the note or history) that's important.

If you want to see the notes and histories entered by a specific user for a group of contacts, the user settings you would want to use are *All users* on the **General** tab and the specific user on the **Note** and **History** tab. If you select the specific user on the **General** tab and the specific user on the **Note** and **History** tabs, you would get the notes and histories entered by that user but **only** for the contacts where that user was the record manager.

Filtering activities in reports

In any report that includes activities, there are special filtering options for the activities. For this task, we will be using the Activities report.

How to do it...

1. From any screen in the ACT! program, click on **Reports** in the navigation bar on the left side of the screen.
2. In the **Report List**, double-click on the **Activities** report.
3. Click the radio button next to **All Contacts**.
4. Check **Exclude 'My Record'**.
5. Click the dropdown for **Send the report output to** and select **Preview**.
6. Click the radio button for **All users**.

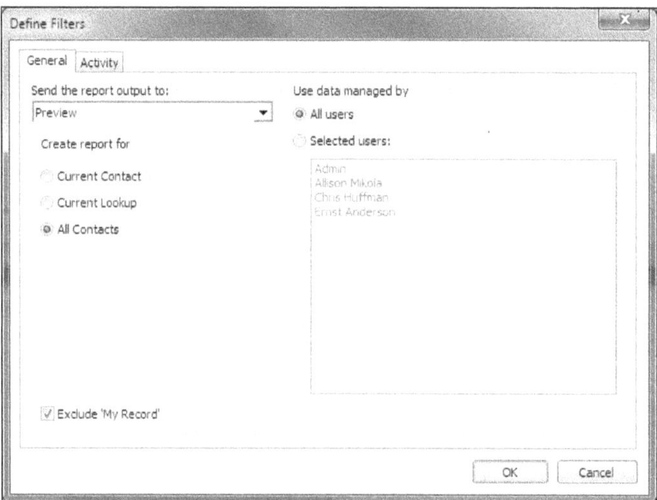

7. Click on the **Activity** tab and follow these steps:
   i. Check **Calls** and **Meetings**.
   ii. Uncheck **To-Do's** and **Custom**.
   iii. Uncheck **include cleared activities**.
   iv. Click the radio button for **All users**
   v. Click the dropdown for **Date range** and select **Next Week**.

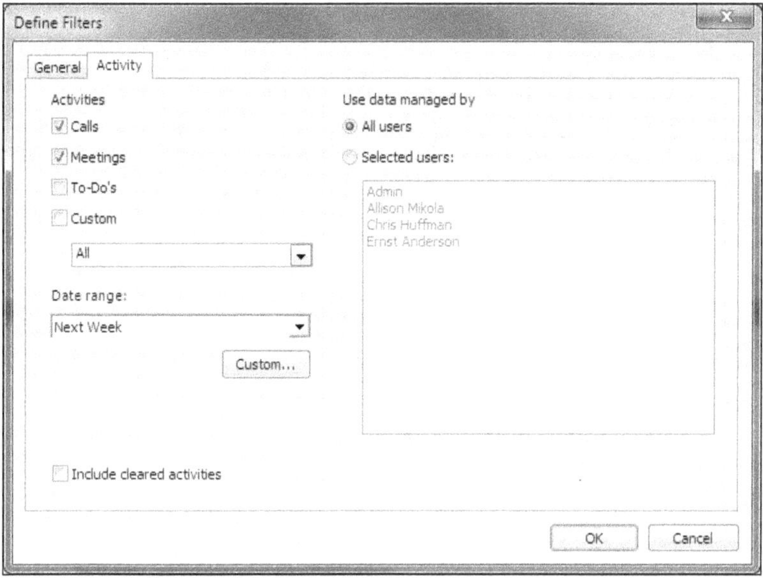

vi. Click **OK** to run the report with these filter options.

How it works...

With the Activities report, the **Define Filters** dialog has an additional tab. Besides the **General** tab there is an **Activity** tab. This tab provides additional filtering for the report. The **General** tab provides filter selections based on the contact record. This is the primary filtering for the report because the filters here decide which contact record to include in the report. Because we selected the **All Contacts filter** option, the report initially will include all the contacts in the database except for the user's My records.

The contact activities have a one-to-many relationship with the contact record so there can be several activity entries linked to the contact record. The Activity tab allows setting additional filters for those records and if no linking records are found the contact will be excluded.

In the **Activity** tab, there are checkboxes that, unchecked, allows excluding specific activity types from the report. When the **Custom** checkbox is unchecked, the associated dropdown is disabled. The Date range filter allows limiting the activities included to a specified date range. The dropdown provides several common date range options and the custom button opens a start and end calendar so that any date range you might need can be specified. The Use data managed by filter allows you to select notes entered by all users, a single user or a combination of users. There is also a checkbox to include or exclude cleared activities.

There's more...

While activities are generally used for planning and keeping appointments, once the activity is completed and cleared, it remains in the database as a cleared activity. The Date Range settings allow you to set either a future date range or a past date range. It would be assumed that when you view a future date range, there wouldn't be any cleared activities. However, if you want to review past activity, you would want to make sure the **Include cleared activity** checkbox was checked.

Filtering Groups reports

The group based reports have a slightly different Define Filters dialog from the one used with the contact reports. It's generally the same but with some slightly different options.

How to do it...

1. From any screen in the ACT! program, click on **Reports** in the navigation bar on the left-hand side of the screen.
2. In the **Report List**, double-click on the **Group Membership** report.
3. Click the radio button next to **All Groups**.
4. Click the dropdown for **Send the report output to** and select **Preview**.
5. Click the radio button for **All users**.

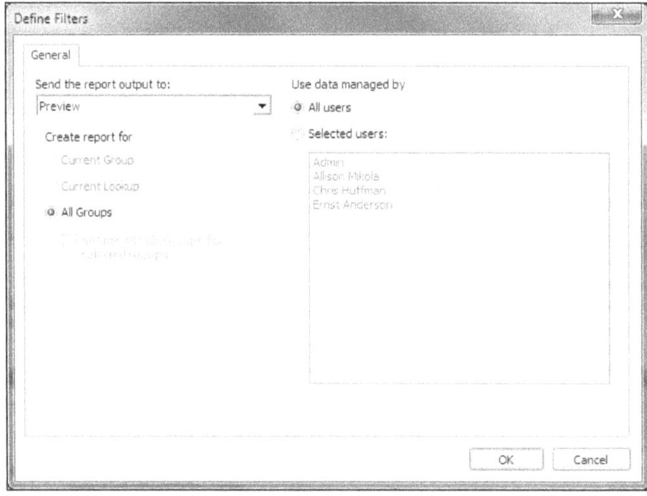

6. Click **OK** to run the report with these filter options.

How it works...

The main difference in the **General** tab filtering for the groups reports is in the **Create report for**. Where the contact reports always allowed you to select any of the three options: Current Contact, Current Lookup, or All Contacts, with the group reports the only option that will be active is the All Groups option, unless you created a lookup of some specific groups prior to launching the report. In the case of the contacts, there is always a lookup of some kind, even if that lookup is all contacts, and there is always an underlying current contact. With the groups, there isn't a default lookup or a default current group. So it's necessary to create a lookup of groups with one of the available queries to activate the group **Create report for** checkboxes. There is an additional checkbox available, when you have a lookup of groups and it's **Include All Sub-Groups for the Selected Groups**. When checked, it causes all the sub-groups for a parent group to be included in the report, even if the sub-groups weren't part of the lookup.

Filtering Company reports

The company based reports have a slightly different Define Filters dialog from the one used with the contact reports. It's generally the same but with some slightly different options.

How to do it...

1. From any screen in the ACT! program, click on **Reports** in the navigation bar on the left-hand side of the screen.
2. In the **Report List**, double click on the **Company Directory** report.
3. Click the radio button next to **All Companies**.
4. Click the dropdown for **Send the report output to** and select **Preview**.
5. Click the radio button for **All users**.

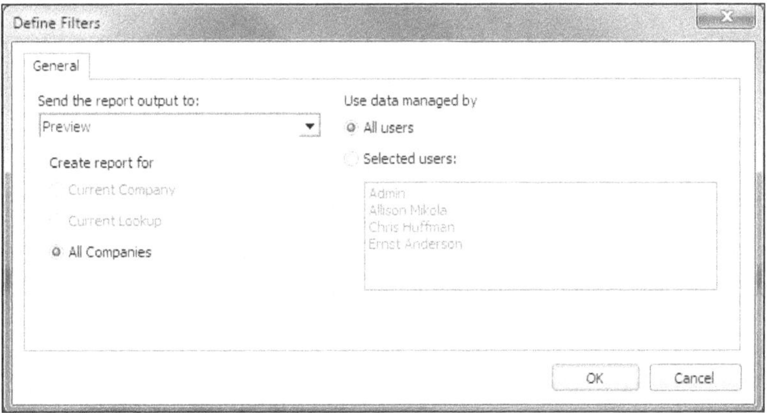

6. Click **OK** to run the report with these filter options.

How it works...

The main difference in the **General** tab filtering for the company reports is in the **Create report for** section. Where the contact reports always allowed you to select any of the three options: Current Contact, Current Lookup, or All Contacts, with the company reports the only option that will be active is All Companies, unless you created a lookup of some specific companies prior to launching the report. In the case of the contacts, there is always a lookup of some kind even if that lookup is all contacts, and there is always an underlying current contact. With the companies there isn't a default lookup or a default current company. To activate the company **Create report for** checkboxes, it's necessary to create a lookup of companies using one of the available queries.

Filtering Opportunity reports

The opportunity based reports have a significantly different Define Filters dialog from the one used with the contact reports. It appears generally the same but there is one significantly different option.

How to do it...

1. From any screen in the ACT! program, click on **Reports** in the navigation bar on the left-hand side of the screen.
2. In the **Report List**, double-click on the **Opportunities by Status** report.
3. In the **Opportunities** section, uncheck **Closed - Lost** and **Inactive**.
4. Click the dropdown for **Date Range** and select **Last Month**.
5. Click the dropdown for **Send the report output to** and select **Preview.**
6. Click the radio button for **All users**.

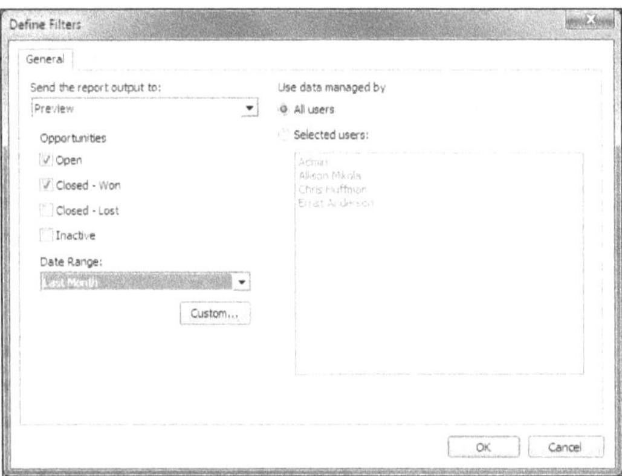

7. Click **OK** to run the report with these filter options.

How it works...

The main difference is the **General** tab filtering, and the differences are significant. Where the contact, groups, and company reports always allowed you to select any of the three options for the number of contacts included in the report, the opportunity based reports have no such options. Now the main selection options are based on the status of the opportunity: **Open, Closed Won, Closed Lost**, or **Inactive** and the date range specified. In the case of open opportunities, the date used for filtering is the Estimated Close Date. For closed opportunities, the Actual Close Date is used.

Presetting filters for most used option

In the previous tasks, we always specified setting all the filter options on the General tab and any secondary tabs. For each of those tasks there were filter options already set, some that we used and some that we had to change. If you always run a specific report with most or all of the same filter settings, it would be an advantage to have those or most of these option settings preset in the report. This is how to do that.

How to do it...

1. From any screen in the ACT! program, click on **Reports** in the navigation bar on the left-hand side of the screen.
2. In the **Report List**, right-click on the **Notes - Histories** report.
3. Click on the **Edit** menu and then on the **Define Filters** option.

4. In **Create report for**, click on the radio button for **Current Contact**.
5. Click on the dropdown for **Send the report output to** and choose **PDF File**.

6. In **Use data managed by**, click the radio button next to **All users**.

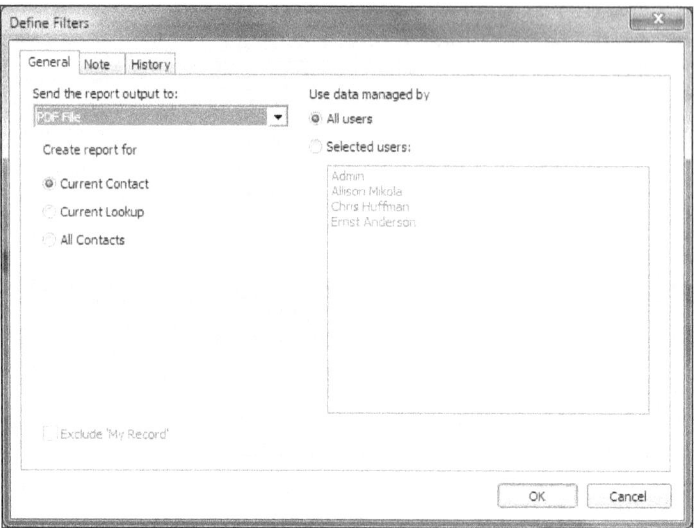

7. Click on the **Note** tab and uncheck **Notes** checkbox.

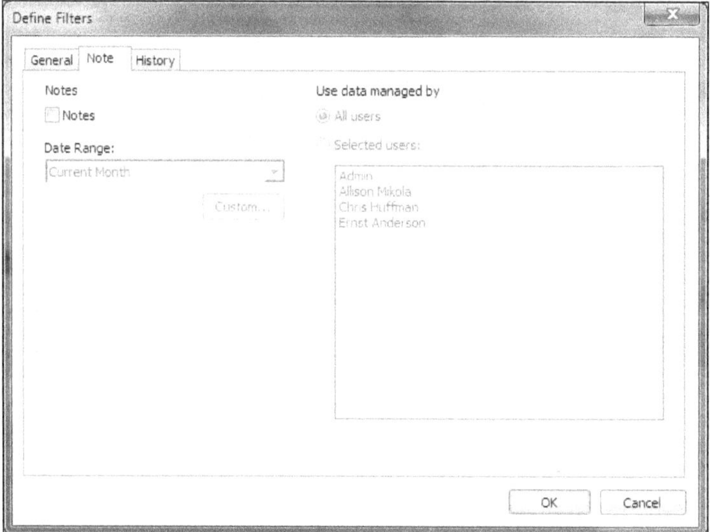

8. Click on the **History** tab an perform the following steps:
   i. In **Histories**, uncheck **Attachments**.
   ii. Click the dropdown in **Date range** and select **Last Month**.
   iii. In **Use data managed by** click the radio button next to **All users**.

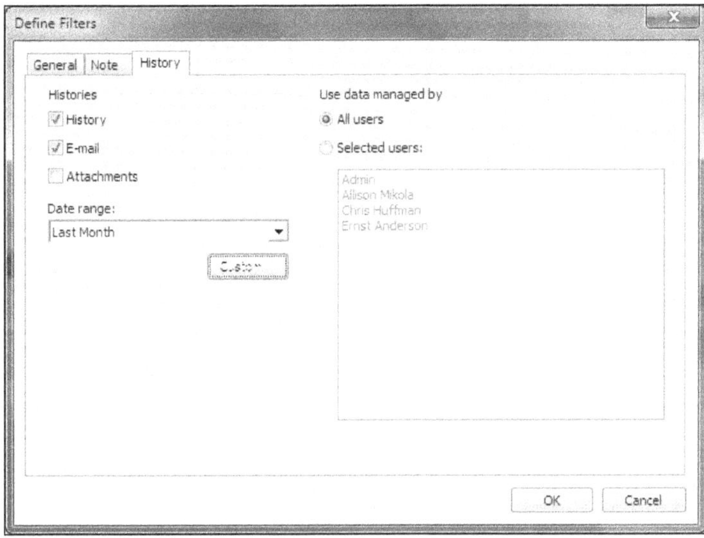

iv. Click the **OK** button to save the filter setting in the report template.

9. Click on the **File** menu and choose **Save As** and name the modified report **My Notes - History**.
10. Close the report editor.

How it works...

In this task, we actually made permanent changes to the report template. The report editor allows for specifying some of the filter settings that are used when you run the report. Some things to notice: when we unchecked the Notes checkbox, all the options on the Note tab were disabled. When the report is run, it will not include any of the notes for the contact. The Date Range used was one of the choices from the dropdown which are all date ranges related to the day the report is run. While a custom date range can be set, it would be fixed and not very useful. All users were specified on all tabs. While user selections seem to be possible when presetting the filters, the settings aren't reliable and the best option is to preset to All users.

3
Creating a Quick Report

In this chapter, we will cover:

- Setting preferences for the quick reports
- Selecting and organizing the columns for a Contact List Quick Report
- Printing the contact list quick report
- Printing a History tab quick report
- Printing the contact detail View quick report
- Exporting the Opportunities List View to Excel

Introduction

The ACT! program provides two different types of reports: **quick reports** and **standard reports**.

The standard report requires that a template be prepared in advance. The template may be brand new, an existing template, or a modified version of an existing template. While the standard report's template design is very flexible, it does require significant effort to design and organize the template. For complex reporting needs or reports that are frequently required, the standard reports are the best.

The Quick reports provide simple reports that require minimum configuration and are easy to run. These reports are either list prints or screen prints with headers and footers to identify the report. The ease of creating a quick report makes them ideal for single use reports. The configuration of a quick report can't be saved so if a quick report configuration is frequently required, you should consider creating a standard report template instead.

The ACT! demo database is used for the tasks in this chapter.

In this chapter we'll be going through the different types for quick reports and configuring the various options for the quick reports.

Setting preferences for the quick reports

The preferences for all the quick reports can be individually set in the ACT! **general preferences**. Unless blocked, they can be set at the time you run the quick report. Here we will set the preferences for the contact list quick reports.

Getting ready

Because we are setting global preferences, there isn't any preparation required other than to have an ACT! database open.

How to do it...

1. From any screen in the ACT! program, click on the **Tools** menu and choose **Preferences...**.
2. In the **Preferences** dialog, click on the **Communication** tab.
3. In the **Printing** section, click on the **Quick Print Preferences...** button.

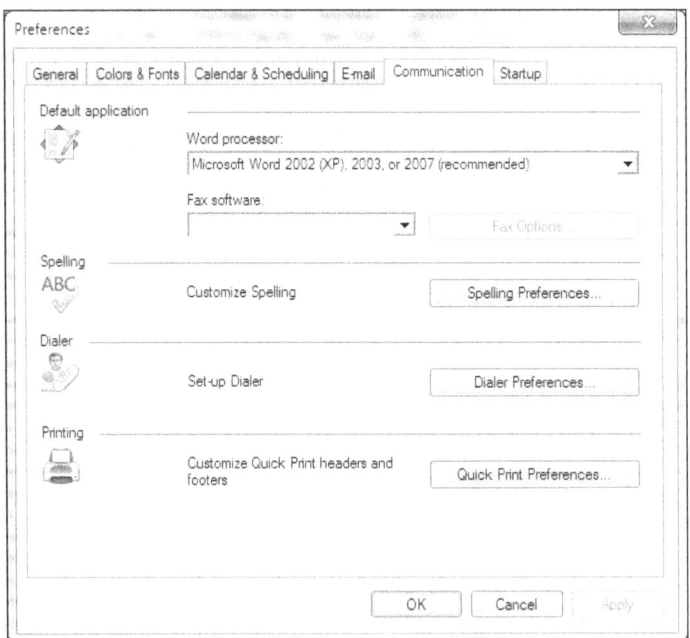

4. In the **Views** section, select **Contact List.**
5. For **Print orientation**, click on the radio button for **Landscape.**
6. For **Print sizing**, click on the radio button for **Actual size.**
7. For **Other options**, check **Same font in my list view**.
8. Check **Show Quick Print Options** when printing.

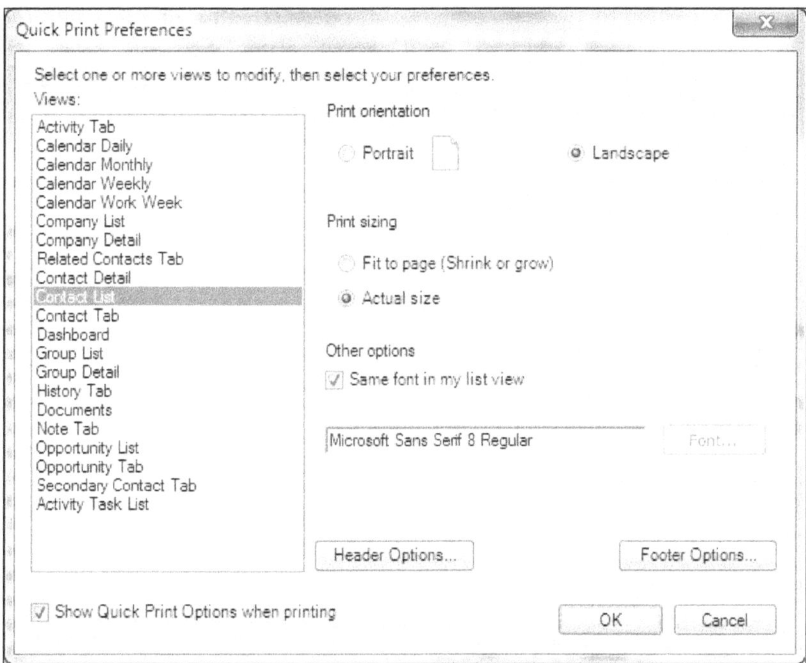

9. Click the **Header Options** button.
10. Check **Page Number**, **Print Date**, **Print Time**, and **My Record**.

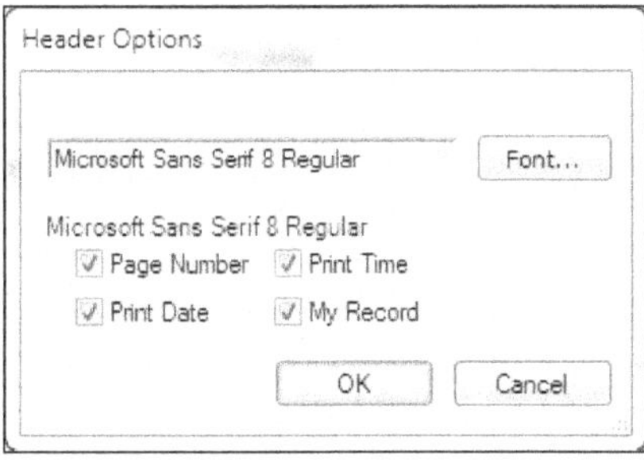

11. Click **OK**.
12. Click **Footer Options** button.

13. Uncheck all options and click **OK**.
14. Click **OK** to close the **Quick Print Preferences** dialog.
15. Click **OK** to close the **Preferences** dialog.

How it works...

At this point, we are setting the general options for the Quick Print reports. In the Quick Print Preferences dialog **Views** section, all of the possible Quick Print report possibilities are shown and each can be configured separately. This task used the **Contact List Quick Report** as an example. The **Portrait - Landscape** option determines the orientation of the printed report. As a general rule the **Print Sizing** option should be set to actual size because the fit to page option shrinks the report both horizontally and vertically to fit on one page. Used with the Contact List Quick Report could result in a final report that was not legible. The font selection would most likely be the same as used on the contact list view, but it does provide for changing the desired font. The header and footer options are the same and typically one or the other would be used but not both. The **My record** option prints the name of the user running the report. The **Show Quick Print** options when printing allow for adjusting the report options when running the report. Unchecked, the report will go directly to the printer.

There's more...

The quick reports don't provide any means for setting the page margins. While the **Fit to page** option should typically be set to **Actual size** for a list view Quick Report, you will likely want to use the **Fit to page** option when doing a Quick Print of a detail view.

Selecting and organizing the columns for a contact list quick report

In this task, we continue working with the Contact List Quick Report. The contact list is able to display all the fields in the contact table. While possible, in most cases this would be impractical. To create a meaningful report you need to decide which fields you want to show in the report. Because you will be printing the contact list, make sure the contact list is showing the fields that you want and that they are arranged in the desired order. In this task we will set up a name and address list.

Getting ready

There isn't any preparation required for the contact list quick report other than having an ACT! database open.

How to do it...

1. In the navigation bar, on the right-hand side of the screen, click on **Contacts**.
2. In the tool bar, click on **List View** button.
3. Anywhere in the **List View**, right-click and select **Customize Columns...**.
4. In the **Customize Columns** dialog, add fields to the list by clicking in the desired field in the **Available fields** box and then clicking the top arrow button (points right **>**).
5. Remove unwanted fields by clicking on the field in the **Show as columns in this order** box and then clicking on the second from the top arrow button (points left **<**).
6. Adjust the order of the fields by clicking on a field in the **Show as columns in this order** box and click on the **Move Up** or **Move Down** buttons to move the field to the desired location.

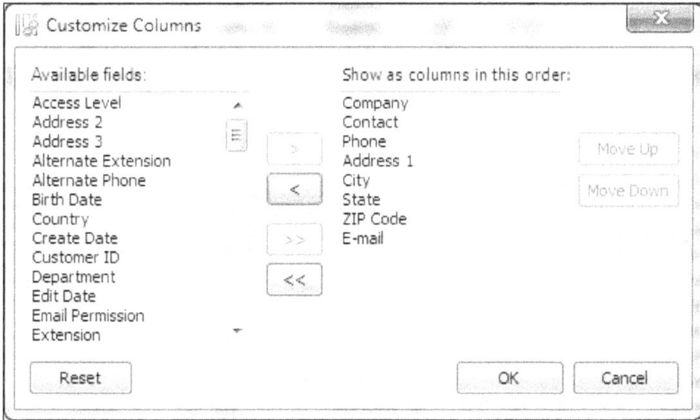

7. Click the **OK** button to close and save the field configuration.
8. In the title bar of the contact list, point the cursor to the division between columns and the cursor becomes a double ended arrow.

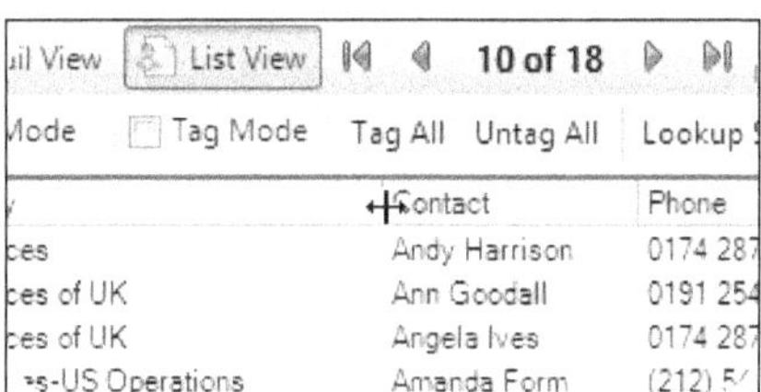

9. Drag the division line to adjust the column width.
10. Adjust the remaining columns in the same manner.

How it works...

Because the quick reports are basically screen image reports, it's necessary to make the screen look the way you want the report to look. For the contact list quick report (and most list reports) this requires selecting the fields (columns) that you want in the report and arranging and sizing them so they look the way you want them to look on the printed report. The **Customize Columns** dialog provides the mechanism for selecting the fields to include and to position them in the desired order. Sizing the columns is a bit harder. The columns divisions can be dragged to widen or narrow a column. The column being sized is the column to the left of the column division.

There's more...

The quick reports don't provide any means for directly filtering the output. The best means of filtering the contacts included in the contact list quick report is to use a lookup of the contacts to include in the report. Refer to the task on filtering based on a lookup in *Chapter 2, Filtering Data in Reports*. You can also apply a simple sort on the contact list by clicking on the column title of the column you want to use for sorting. Each time you click on the column title, you reverse the sort order.

Printing the contact list quick report

In this task, we continue working with the contact list quick report, moving now to the actual printing of the report.

Getting ready

If you want to print a specific group of contacts, you should create a lookup of those contacts prior to running the report. For this task, I made a lookup of all the contacts in the ACT! Demo database where the city name started with *New*. I also did a sort on the **City** column.

How to do it...

1. In the **Contact** screen **| List View**, click the **File** menu and select **Quick Print Current Window**.

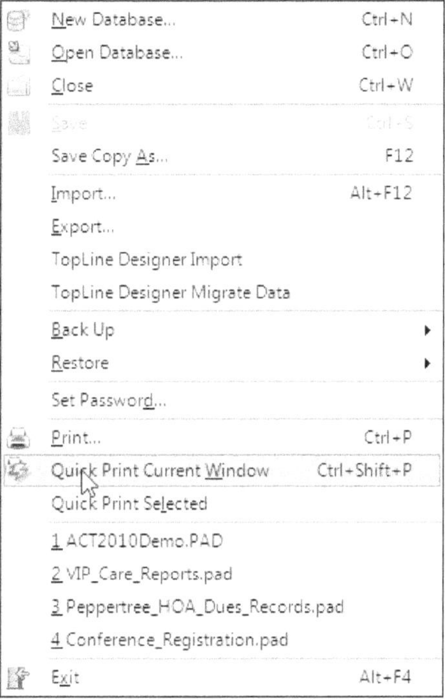

2. In the **Quick Print Option**s dialog, **Print orientation**, click the radio button for **Landscape**.
3. In **Print sizing**, click the radio button for **Actual size**.
4. In **Other options**, uncheck **Same font in my list view** and click the **Font...** button.
5. In the **Font** dialog, choose **Times New Roman**.
6. For the **Font style**, choose **Regular**.
7. For the **Size**, choose **10**.

8. Click the **OK** button to save the font selection.

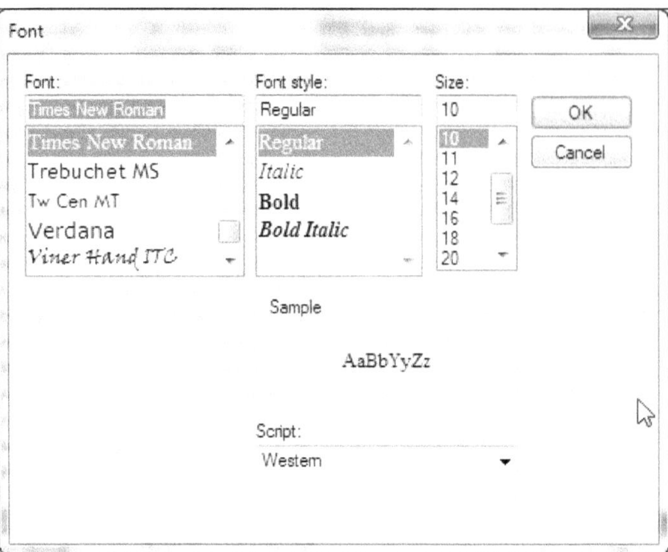

9. Click the **OK** button to open the **Quick Print Options** dialog.

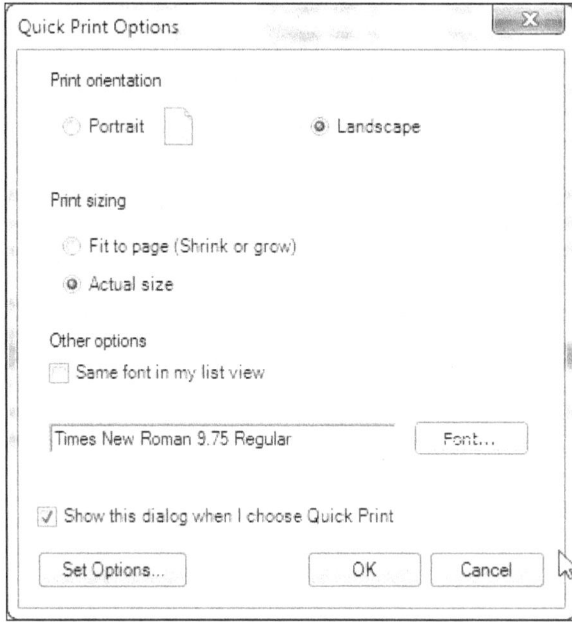

10. Select print options applicable for your printer and click the **OK** button to print the report.

How it works...

The list print quick reports print what is listed on the screen with the addition of a simple header or footer. If the list is very long, for example, and you did all contacts for the lookup, the quick report would print a multiple page report that would include contacts that were valid for the lookup but didn't fit on the viable screen.

There's more...

The File menu also had a selection for Quick Print Selected. This allows you to select some of the contacts that are in the list view by tagging the contacts and then print only those records. This is useful if you needed to print a few records out of a lookup without losing the lookup. This particular option is more useful when doing a Quick Print of a tab such as **history** or **notes**.

Printing the History tab quick report

In this task, we are working with the **History Tab Quick Report** on the contact detail screen. The quick reports for the various tabs are useful when you want a hard copy of the Notes, History, Activity, or Opportunity records for a contact.

Getting ready

You need to navigate to the contact detail screen, select the desired contact, and then click the History tab on the screen, to display the history for that contact. The **History** tab allows for the selection of the columns displayed and the sizing of the columns. This process is very similar to the process used with the **Contact List** and needs to be done before printing the report. The **History** tab does allow for filtering what needs to be set up.

How to do it...

1. In the **History** filter bar, set **Dates** to **All Dates**.
2. Click the dropdown for **Types** and check **Histories** and **E-mails**.
3. Click on **Select users**.

4. In the **Select users** dialog, click on the radio button for **All users**.

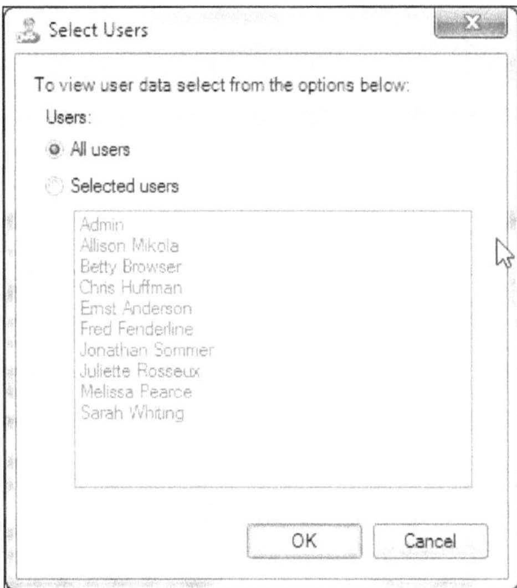

5. Click the **OK** button to save the selection.
6. Click the **File** menu and select **Quick Print Selected**.

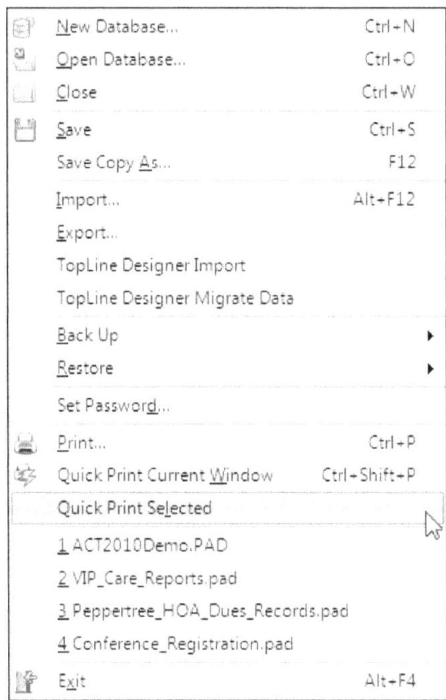

7. In the **Quick Print Options** dialog click the radio button for **Landscape** for the **Print orientation**.
8. For **Print sizing** click the radio button for **Actual size**.
9. Check **Same font in my list view** for the **Other options**.
10. Click the **OK** button to open the Print dialog.
11. Select print options applicable for your printer and click the **OK** button to print the report.

How it works...

The main difference here from the contact list quick report is the filtering that's available in the tab view. This filtering applies to the specific tab but does stay the same when you move to another contact. The other difference is that it's important to choose Quick Print Selected. The Quick Print Current window would include the upper part of the screen and would only include the history actually visible on the screen.

There's more...

There's a bit of a trick to make sure you get what you want in the report. The steps in this task ensure you will print all the history you have filtered for, even if it extends beyond the bottom of the screen. If you select any of the history records and run the report for **selected**, only the highlighted histories will print. By going through the filters and then running Quick Print Selected, all of the histories will print.

Printing the contact detail view quick report

The previous quick reports were all list view reports. The ACT! program has the ability to do a quick report of a detail screen, in effect doing a print screen. In this task, we will do a contact detail view quick report.

Getting ready

The main reason to do a quick report of the contact detail view is to print out a hard copy of the main information related to a single contact. Before running the quick report you need to do a lookup so that the contact whose information you want to print is the current contact. The main contact information is in the upper part of the screen but you will need to select a tab for the bottom part of the detail views.

How to do it...

1. Click on the **Personal Info** tab to display the home address and other information on the bottom part of the screen.
2. Click the **File** menu and select the **Quick Print Current Window**.
3. For **Print orientation** in the **Quick Print Options** dialog, click the radio button for **Landscape**.
4. For **Print sizing**, click on the radio button for **Fit to page (Shrink or grow)**.

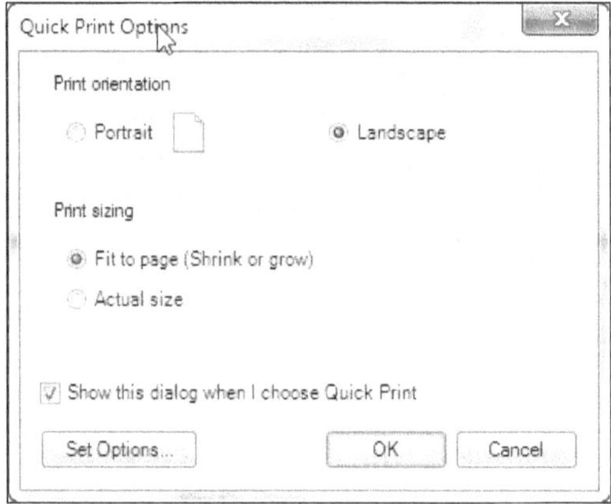

5. Click the **OK** button to open the print dialog.
6. Select print options applicable for your printer and click the **OK** button to print the report.

How it works...

For the detail view quick reports, the ACT! window in the computer screen buffer is captured without the navigation bar at the left of the screen and the toolbars and menus at the top of the screen. When doing a detail view quick report, it's a good idea to choose the **Fit to page** option to avoid multiple pages printing. Also the font option is missing from the Quick Print Options dialog because this report isn't text based as the list view quick reports are.

Exporting the Opportunities List View to Excel

While not actually a quick report, many of the list views in the ACT! program can be directly exported to Excel. Once in Excel, some list views such as the Opportunity List View can be further formatted for presentation. This task will go through the steps to export the Opportunity List View to Excel.

Getting ready

There isn't any preparation required for the export to Excel other than having an ACT! database open.

How to do it...

1. From anywhere in the ACT! program, click on **Opportunities** in the navigation bar on the left-hand side of the screen.
2. In the filter bar at the top of the opportunity list view, use the **Dates** dropdown to select **Past**.
3. Use the **Status** dropdown and check only **Open**.
4. Use the **Process** dropdown to select **CHT1 Sales**.
5. Use the **Stage** dropdown and uncheck all stages except **Commitment to Buy**.
6. Click on the **Probability** radio button for **All**.
7. Click on the **Total** radio button for **All**.
8. Click on the **Select Users** button.
9. Click on the radio button for **All users** in the **Select Users** dialog.
10. Click on the **OK** button to save the setting and close the dialog.

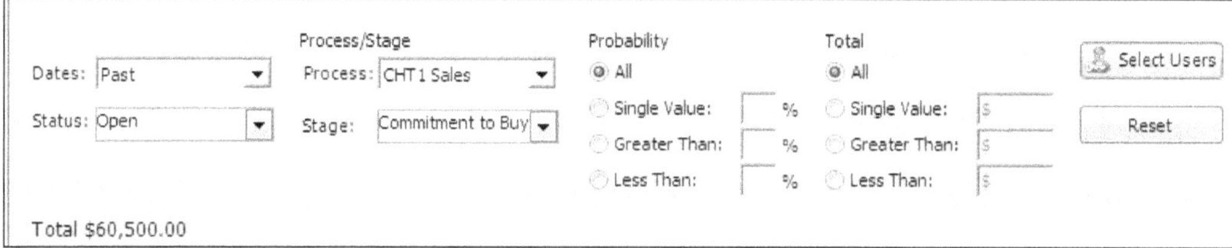

11. Click on the **Export Current List to Excel** icon on the tool bar.

12. View the exported list in Excel.

	A	B	C	D	E	F	G
1	Contact	Company	Status	Record Manager	Opportunity Name	Stage	Total
2	Chris Huffman	CH TechONE	Open	Chris Huffman	New Opportunity	Commitment to Buy	$.00
3	Amanda Form	A1 Services-US Operations	Open	Chris Huffman	A1 Services US Operations-New York Offices	Commitment to Buy	$2,000.00
4	Hayleigh Frieda	American Dreams	Open	Chris Huffman	American Dreams-Upgrade to Main Office	Commitment to Buy	$2,500.00
5	UR Powerful	Captains of Industry	Open	Chris Huffman	COI-Upgrade for Houston	Commitment to Buy	$8,000.00
6	Stony Brooke	Duke Industries	Open	Allison Mikola	Duke Industries-LA Operations	Commitment to Buy	$12,000.00
7	Morty Manicotti	Corleone's Pasta Company	Open	Allison Mikola	Corleone's Pasta-Ovens	Commitment to Buy	$12,000.00
8	John Guild	Continental Detective Agency	Open	Allison Mikola	Continental Detective Agency-Butte Offices	Commitment to Buy	$12,000.00
9	Ethan Turnbull	F G Landscape & Design	Open	Allison Mikola	FG Landscape & Design-2nd Greenhouse	Commitment to Buy	$12,000.00
10							$60,500.00

How it works...

The filters are the ones you would use to narrow down the data you wanted to analyze. The export to Excel feature is built into the ACT! program and isn't limited to Opportunities. Most list views can be exported as shown here.

Important note: All currency columns are automatically totaled as part of the export.

4
Working with the Report Editor

In this chapter, we will cover the following topics:

- Converting ACT! 6 custom reports
- Choosing a template type and setting defaults
- Adding fields to template and basic formatting
- Naming field objects and individual field formatting
- Positioning fields and labels
- Adding a custom field and creating a basic script
- Adding sections for sorting and grouping
- Using sections for sub-totaling and totaling

Introduction

In this chapter, we will be working with the ACT! report editor. We won't be covering the running of the reports here other than for testing purposes. We will 'go under the hood' to look at how to create and customize report templates and good practices for creating the report templates. The converting of custom report templates from the ACT! 3-6 versions of the ACT! program is included.

Newcomers to a reporting tool such as the ACT! Reports often try to view the report template as being similar to a word processing document. Reports are very different from word processing documents. With a word processing document you are working directly with the final output or with a master document that can be edited before printing. With report editors such as the ACT! Reports, you are actually *writing a program* (called a report template), the purpose of which is to extract specific data from a database and format the data for display or printing. The report template can also include instructions to do things like perform arithmetic functions on the data included in the report.

After reading this chapter, you will be able to use the tools provided by the ACT! report editor to create many of the reports that you may need. The first task is converting any custom ACT! 3-6 templates you may have. If you don't need or have already done the report conversion, you can skip the first task.

The remaining tasks in this chapter need to be done in the sequence presented. In fact, each of these tasks use the results of the previous task to build on. While the report template created in this chapter can be run, it isn't intended to be a practical report. The intent of this chapter is to show report design techniques.

Converting ACT! 6 custom reports

Converting the ACT! 3-6 report templates is required only if you have created custom report templates in the earlier version. Most of the standard report templates from the earlier version are automatically available in the later ACT! versions. In most cases, you will do the report template conversion right after you have converted your ACT! 3-6 database.

Getting ready

You need to have the database open where you want to use the converted report templates, because the converted report templates are directly added to that database. If you installed the ACT! program on the same computer where ACT! 6 was installed, the old report templates will be readily available. If this is a different computer, you will need to make sure that the ACT! 6 report templates were copied to a folder in this system.

How to do it...

1. From any screen in the ACT! program, click on the **Tools** menu and select **Convert ACT! 3.0 - 6.0 Items...**.
2. In the dialog, click on **Report Templates**.

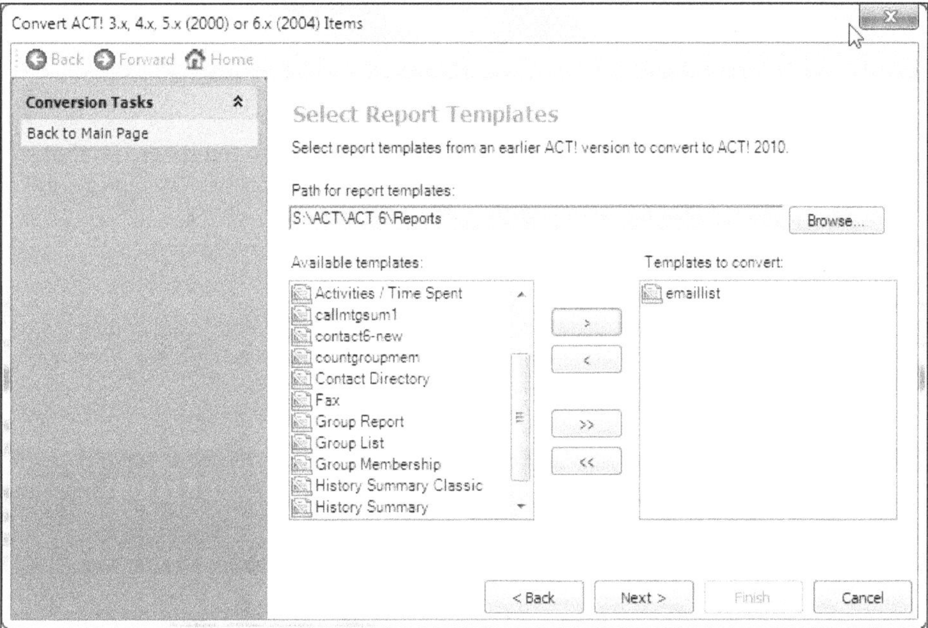

3. If required, click on the **Browse...** button and navigate to the folder where the ACT! 3-6 reports are located.
4. In the **Available templates** box, click on a custom report to convert.
5. Click on the **>** button to move the report to the **Templates to convert** box.
6. Repeat steps 4 and 5 for each custom report you need to convert.
7. Click the **Next** button to start the conversion.
8. When **Conversion Finished** is displayed, click the **Finish** button.
9. Click the **Close** button to exit conversion.

How it works...

The actual conversion process is an internal function of the ACT! program. What is required in this task is locating the ACT! 3-6 Reports and identifying the reports you want to convert.

There's more...

ACT! 3-6 stored the report templates separately from the database and if you had more than one database, the same report templates were shared by all the databases. Now the report templates are stored as part of the database supplemental files so that each database has its own set of report templates. While it's possible to copy report templates from one database to another, they often won't work correctly on the second database. It's best to consider the report templates as being specific to the database where they were created.

In many cases, the converted report will require some additional editing. As a general rule, the required editing will be minor. The following tasks will provide information on how to do the editing.

Choosing a template type and setting defaults

You have decided that you need a report that provides some analysis of the data in your database. You've checked the standard ACT! Reports and none of them fit your exact needs. It is a report that you will need on a regular basis so you need to create a report template for that purpose. The first task in the process is choosing the basic type for the report and setting the defaults for the report.

Getting ready

Starting the process can be done from any screen in the ACT! program using the report menu but the easy way is to start from the report screen.

How to do it...

1. From any screen in the ACT! program, click on **Reports** in the navigation bar on the left-hand side of the screen.
2. Click on **New Report Template**.
3. In the **New Report** dialog, click on **Contact Reports | Empty Contact Report**.

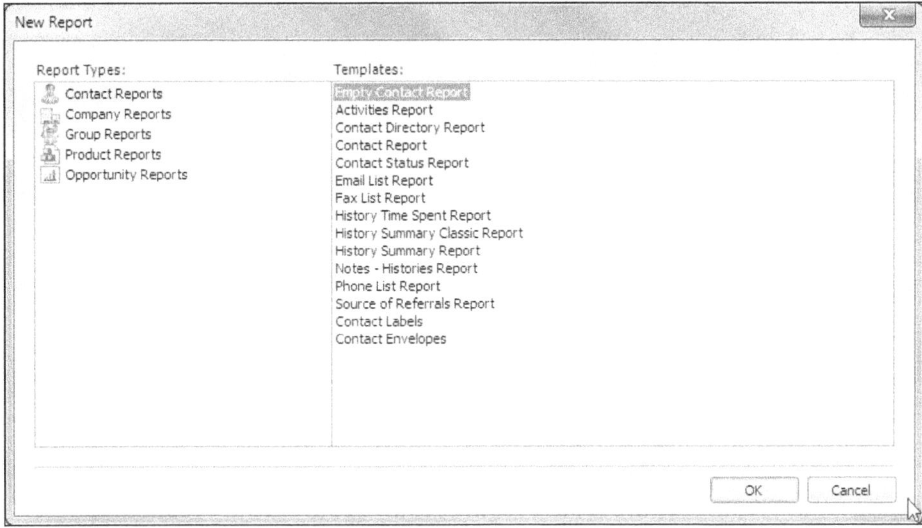

4. Click the **OK** button to open the new report.
5. If the **Properties** panel isn't showing on the right-hand side of the screen, press the *F4* function key.
6. In the field at the top of the **Properties** panel, click on the dropdown and select **Report Template1 Report**.
7. Click on the **Font** property and then the button at the end of the field.
8. In the **Font** dialog, select **Tahoma** for the **Font**, **Regular** for the **Font style** and, **8** for the size.

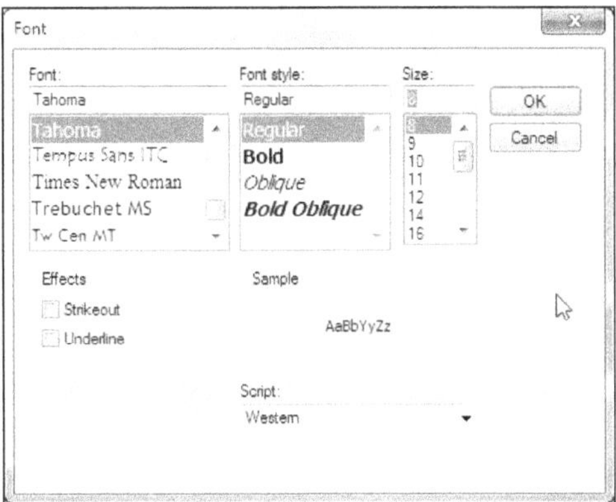

9. Click the **OK** button to save the font settings
10. For **Maximum Pages** specify 0.

11. In the **Layout** section, set all the margins to `0.25`.
12. Set the **Orientation** to **Portrait**.

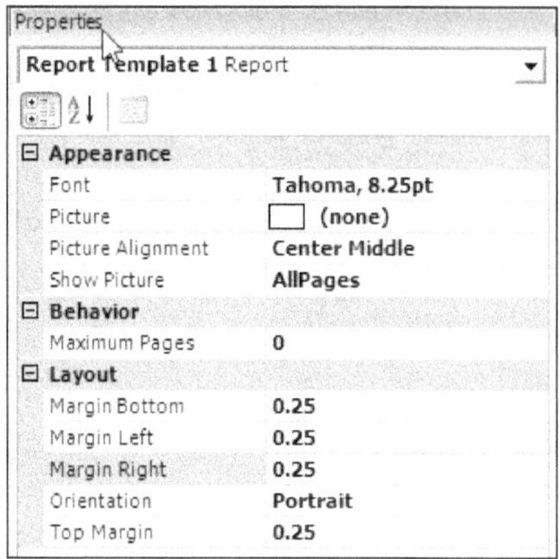

13. Click the **File menu** and select **Save As...**.
14. For the **File Name**, type `Report Training.rep`.
15. Click the **Save** button to save the report.

How it works...

In this task, we started a new contact report template. For this, we wanted a blank template which was done by selecting **Empty Contact Report** for the new template. In this and the following tasks, you will make use of the **Properties** panel for most of the formatting. To minimize future editing, you want to set the font and type size you will use for most fields. We set the margins to maximize the area available on the page to create the template. All the fields that are used in the report template are placed in the exact location that you want. This is unlike a word processor where you use a tab line to establish text positioning.

There's more...

New Report dialog with **Contact Reports** showed a list of all the standard ACT! contact reports. Selecting a different report type would have listed all the standard reports for that report type. If you want to modify a standard report, the best practice is to launch a copy of the standard report from the **New Report** dialog and then do a **Save As** to save the report with a different name.

Unless the changes are minor, I discourage trying to modify the standard reports. Most of the standard reports have hidden fields and added programming scripts and unless you fully research the report template, the modifications can result in an unworkable report template.

Adding fields to template and basic formatting

In the previous task, we started a new report template and set the page and basic text defaults. We saved the template as **Report Training**. Now we will add fields to this training report. We will be setting up a name and address block for this purpose because it includes many of the techniques required to successfully create a workable report.

Getting ready

If you are doing this task immediately after finishing the previous task, you should still have the Report Training template open for editing. If so, skip to step 3. Otherwise start at step 1.

How to do it...

1. From any screen in the ACT! program, click on **Reports** in the navigation bar on the left-hand side of the screen.
2. In the list of report templates, right-click on the **Report Training** template and select **Edit Report**.
3. In the **Toolbox** panel, click on the **Field** tool.
4. Position the field cross hair in the **Detail** section at about one and a half inches from the left-hand side and click and drag down and to the right to create a box about one-inch long.
5. In the **Select Field** dialog, make sure **Select a record type** is set to **Contact** and then double-click on the following fields:
    - **ContactID**
    - **Contact**
    - **Company**
    - **Address 1**
    - **Address 2**
    - **Address 3**
    - **City**

- **State**
- **ZIP Code**

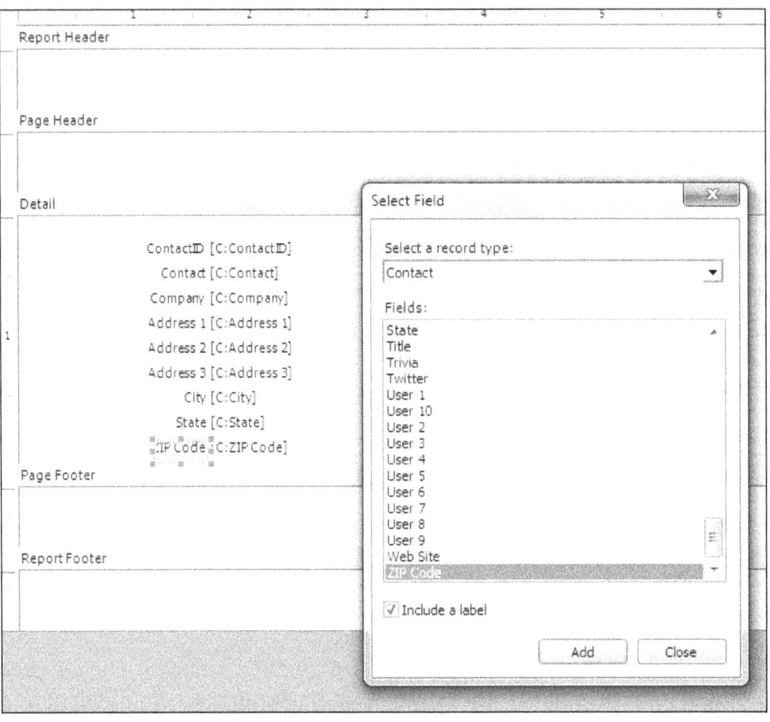

6. Click the **Close** button to close the dialog.
7. Right-click on the **Detail** section bar and choose **Select All**.
8. In the **Properties** panel (press *F4* function key to display) and set **Word Wrap** to **No**.
9. In the **Layout** area set **Alignment** to **Left Middle**.
10. In the **Layout** area set **Height** to `0.14`.
11. Click in the blank area of the **Detail** section then click on the **ContactID** label.
12. Hold down the *Shift* key and left-click once on each of the other field labels.
13. In the **Properties** panel, **Layout** area, set **Left** to `0.05`.
14. Set the **Width** to `0.90`.

15. In the **Font** toolbar, click the **B** to make the field labels bold.

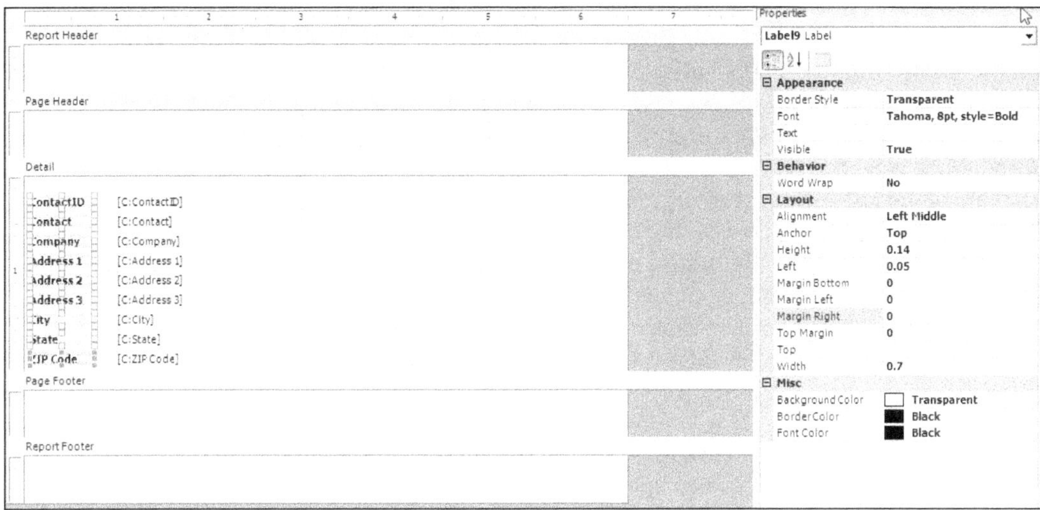

16. Click on the **C:ContactID** field.
17. Hold down the *Shift* key and left-click once on each of the other **C:** fields.
18. In the **Properties** panel **Behavior** area set **Can Grow** to **No**.
19. In the **Layout** area set **Left** to `1.0`.

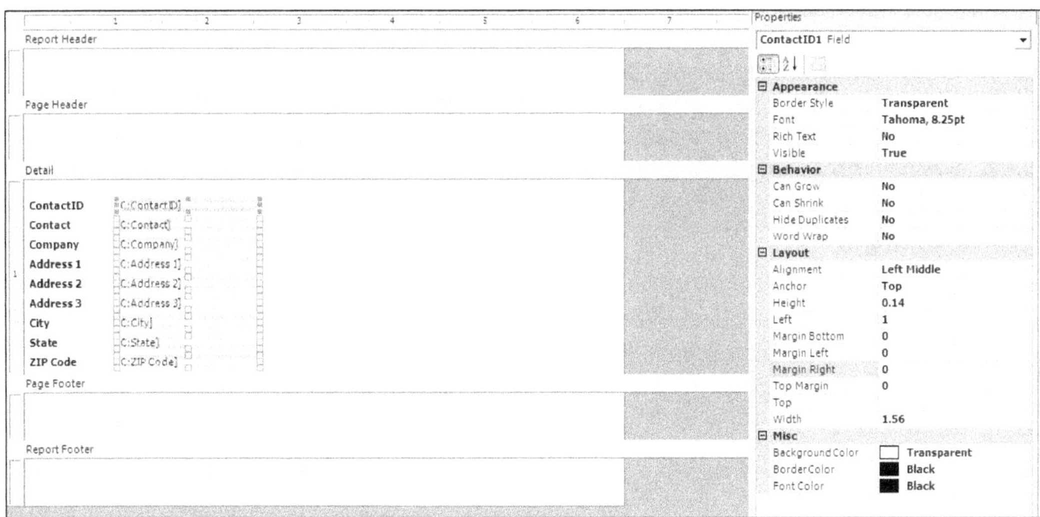

20. Click the **File** menu and select **Save**.

How it works...

These tasks are aimed at showing good practices and productive ways to work with the ACT! Reports. When you add fields to an ACT! report template, the report editor generally uses a default size for the field and the label. This makes efforts to position and size the fields of little value. It's better to simply start adding the fields that you need as a block of fields. Once you have a group of fields to work with, the next thing is to do some preliminary formatting. Because the behavior of most fields will be generally static, it's best to start with all behaviors set to **No**. Likewise the height of the fields should be set for the type size you're using. Because the field labels start out as just large enough for the field name, you want to increase the width and setting of any other characteristics of the labels such as bold, italics, or underscore. Finally move the fields and labels to the approximate location on the template layout where you want them.

Using consistent values for sizing and placement keeps the final report from having a jumbled appearance. For horizontal spacing, let us separate objects by 0.05 inches. This includes starting 0.05 inches from the left margin.

There's more...

In this task, we can select groups of objects, either fields or labels by using the shift-click because it is easier to describe. The ACT! report editor also supports 'lassoing' objects to select them. This is done by clicking and holding with the cursor in a blank part of the template and then dragging at an angle to show a selection box. When the mouse button is released any template objects within or touching the selection box will be selected. Because it's hard to be specific on how to select specific object using lassoing, let us continue to use the more specific method of using shift-click.

Field sizing

Field sizing is critical to the appearance of the report template output. In most cases, you will need to experiment to determine the appropriate width of fields to display the relevant data. However, field height is directly related to the point size of the type you're using. A chart has been created for sizing field heights relative to the point size and this is shown as follows:

Line Height (based on 120% type size in points)		
Type Size in Points	**Height - English**	**Height - Metric**
8	.14	.34
9	.15	.39
10	.17	.42
11	.19	.47
12	.2	.51
14	.24	.6
16	.27	.68
18	.3	.77
20	.34	.85

Naming field objects and individual field formatting

If you have past experience with visual programming editors such as Visual Basic, the tools in the ACT! report editor should be somewhat familiar. As with visual programming editors, everything in the ACT! report template has an object name. When you insert a field or field label, the report editor assigns a default name to the element that is called the object name. In most cases, the default name is fine. However, as the template becomes more complex, the default field names become inadequate. This happens because the default field names are based on the database field name. As the list of objects becomes longer, it can be difficult to find specific fields. In the previous task, we did most of the field formatting but now we need to do some specific field formatting.

Getting ready

If you are doing this task immediately after finishing the previous task, you should still have the Report Training template open for editing. If so, skip to step 3. Otherwise start at step 1.

How to do it...

1. From any screen in the ACT! program, click on **Reports** in the navigation bar on the left-hand side of the screen.
2. In the list of report templates, right-click on the **Report Training** template and select **Edit Report**.
3. Click on the **C:ContactID** field.

4. In the **Properties** panel (press *F4* function key to display), **Misc** area set the name to **FContactID1**.

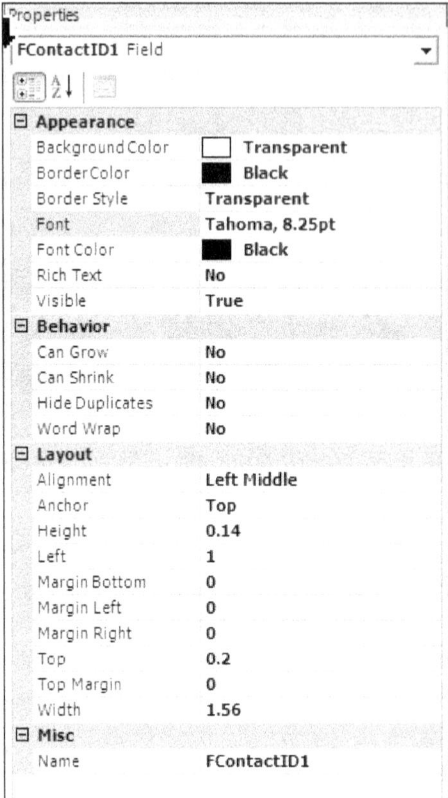

5. In turn, starting with the **C:Contact** field, click on and rename each of the **C:** field objects by adding an `F` to the beginning of the default name.
6. Click on the **C:ContactID** field.
7. In the **Properties** panel, **Appearance** area, set **Visible** to **False**.
8. In the **Layout** area, set **Height** to `0.01`, **Width** to `0.15`, **Left** to `7.75`, and **Top** to `0.01`.

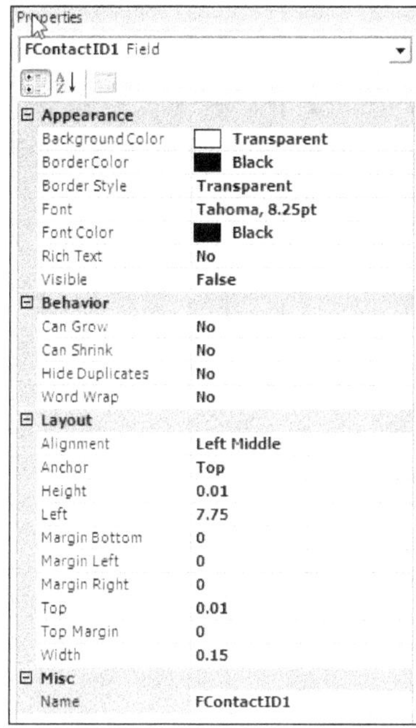

9. Click on the **City** label.
10. In the **Properties** panel, **Appearance** area, set **Text** to **City State Zip**.
11. Delete the labels **ContactID**, **State**, and **ZIP Code**.

12. Click the **File** menu and select **Save**.

How it works...

We did two important things in this task. The first was to establish a naming convention for the field object in the template. The ACT! program provides a unique default name for all of the field objects added to the template based on the database field name. If left unchanged, the field objects are hard to find in the alphabetic listing of template objects in the Properties panel. You can use any naming convention that you want, or none if you choose. It's better to add the *F* for field to the start of each field object name so the fields will be grouped together in the object list.

The second thing we did was to reformat the **C:ContactID** field and hide it. The **C:ContactID** field contains the unique ID for the record. The record's unique ID is critical for proper linking of the records in the main table with the records in any sub-reports added to the report template. The best way is adding this field to the report and hiding it for future use. Because the **ContactID** label was no longer needed, we deleted it along with the State and ZIP Code labels. We will be creating a custom field in a later task to concatenate the City, State, and ZIP Code fields.

There's more...

We did a simple rename of the object names in this task, and it may seem like a waste of time. The importance of the object name and having a good naming convention becomes important when you get into enhancing a report template with **Visual Basic** (**VB**) script programming. When naming objects you can't use any spaces and do not use the math symbols + _ * / =. These cause problems with the script interpreter.

Positioning fields and labels

In an earlier task, we sized and did the horizontal positioning for the fields and their labels. In the previous task, we removed unwanted labels and hid the **C:ContactID** field for later use. Now we will do the vertical placement of the fields and labels.

Getting ready

If you are doing this task immediately after finishing the previous task, you should still have the Report Training template open for editing. If so, skip to step 3. Otherwise start at step 1.

How to do it...

1. From any screen in the ACT! program, click on **Reports** in the navigation bar on the left-hand side of the screen.
2. In the list of report templates right-click on the **Report Training template** and select **Edit Report**.

3. Click on the **Contact** label, hold down the *Shift* key and click on the **C:Contact** field.
4. In the **Properties** panel, **Layout** area, set **Top** to `0.02`.

5. Click on the **Company** label, hold down the *Shift* key, and click on the **C:Company** field.
6. In the **Properties** panel, **Layout** area, set **Top** to `0.18`.

Calculate the proper Top setting by taking the Top setting for the contact line (0.02), adding the contact line field height (0.14), and then adding the desired line spacing (0.02). Thus 0.02+0.14+0.02=0.18.

7. Click on the **Address 1** label, hold down the *Shift* key, and click on the **C:Address1** field.
8. In the **Properties** panel, **Layout** area, set **Top** to `0.34`.
9. Click on the **Address 2** label, hold down the *Shift* key, and click on the **C:Address2** field.
10. In the **Properties** panel, **Layout** area, set **Top** to `0.50`.
11. Click on the **Address 3** label, hold down the *Shift* key, and click on the **C:Address3** field.
12. In the **Properties** panel, **Layout** area, set **Top** to `0.66`.
13. Click on the **City State ZIP** label.

14. In the **Properties** panel, **Layout** area, set **Top** to `0.82`.

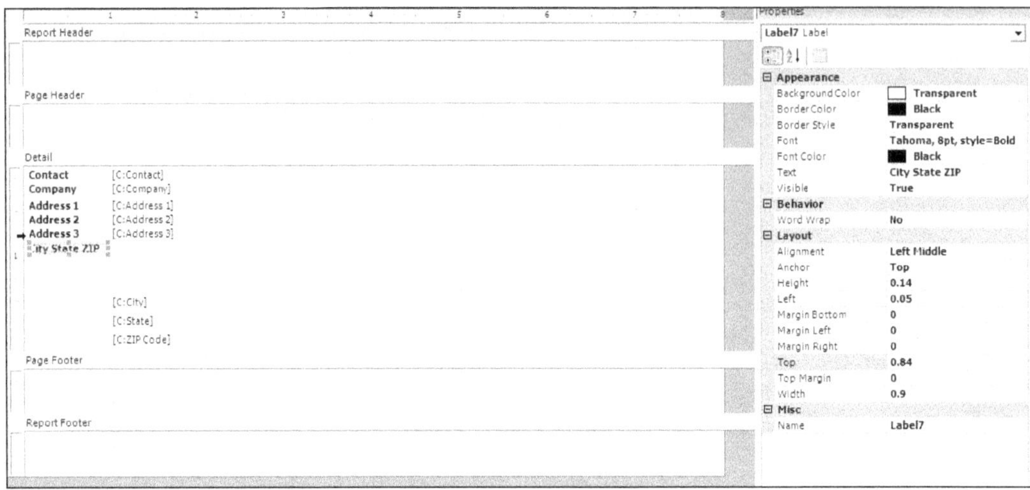

15. Click the **File** menu and select **Save**.

How it works...

In a previous task, we did the horizontal positioning of the label and field object in blocks. For the vertical positioning, we need to do the positioning one line at a time. For both horizontal and vertical positioning, the location needs to be calculated based on the object dimensions and the space you want to have between the objects. In this task, we didn't position the **C:City**, **C:State**, or **C:ZIP** Code fields. These fields will be positioned in the next task.

There's more...

There is a selection trick that we will be using later. Place the cursor in the left margin of the template workspace adjacent to a row objects you want to select and then click the left mouse button. All objects in the row will be selected. In fact you can click and drag to select multiple rows of objects at the same time.

Adding a custom field and creating a basic script

The ACT! report editor doesn't provide any means of automatically concatenating field objects such as typically is done for the city, state, and ZIP code line in an address. If the field objects are simply positioned on the line, there will be unwanted gaps between the address data. To provide the proper concatenation a custom field and a simple VB Program script is used.

Getting ready

If you are doing this task immediately after finishing the previous task, you should still have the Report Training template open for editing. If so, skip to step 3. Otherwise start at step 1.

How to do it...

1. From any screen in the ACT! program, click on **Reports** in the navigation bar on the left-hand side of the screen.
2. In the list of report templates right-click on the **Report Training** template and select **Edit Report**.
3. In the **Toolbox** panel, click on the **System Field** tool.
4. Position the field cross hair in the **Detail** section at about one and a half inches from the left side and below the address field objects. Click and drag down and to the right to create a box about one inch long.
5. In the **Select System Field** dialog, uncheck the **Include a label** option.
6. Double-click on the **Custom** field.
7. Click the **Close** button.
8. Click on the **Custom** field you inserted.
9. In the **Properties** panel, **Layout** area, set **Left** to `1.0`, **Heights** to `0.14`, **Top** to `0.82`, and **Width** to `2.0`.
10. The default object name should be **Custom1**. Make note of the exact spelling.
11. Click in turn on the **C:City**, **C:State**, and **C:ZIP** Code fields and take not of the exact spelling of the object names.
12. Left-click on the **Detail** bar and then right-click and select **Edit Report Scripts**.
13. In the **Edit Report Scripts** dialog, confirm that the **OnPrint** type of script is selected.

14. In the dialog workspace, type the following:

```
Custom1.text = FCity1&", "&FState1&" "&FZIPCode1
```

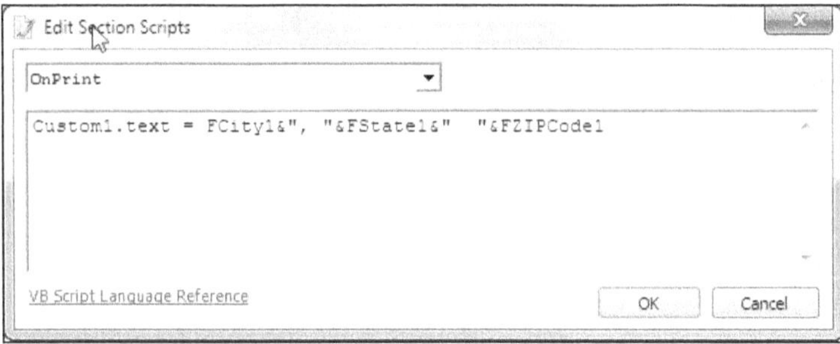

15. Click the **OK** button.
16. Test the script by clicking the **File** menu and selecting **Print Preview**.
17. Close the **Print Preview** screen.
18. Click on the **C:City** field and set the **Appearance Visible** property to **False**.
19. Set the **Layout Width** property to `0.15`, the **Height property** to `0.01`, the **Left** property to `7.75` and the **Top** property to `0.03`.
20. Click on the **C:State** field and set the **Appearance Visible** property to **False.**
21. Set the **Layout Width** property to `0.15`, the **Height property** to `0.01`, the **Left** property to `7.75`, and the **Top** property to `0.05`.
22. Click on the **C:ZIPCode** field and set the **Appearance Visible** property to **False.**
23. Set the **Layout Width** property to `0.15`, the **Height** property to `0.01`, the **Left** property to `7.75`, and the **Top** property to `0.07`.
24. Click on the **Detail** bar.
25. Set the **Height** property to `1.0`.

26. Click the **File** menu and select **Save**.

How it works...

Custom fields are classed as system fields in that they don't directly connect to a database field but rather serve as the target for a VB program script. Custom fields are inserted, formatted, and positioned the same way as a data field. The program script here is very simple consisting of one line of programming. Going into the program language syntax is beyond the scope of this document.

There's more...

If you want more information on the VB script programming syntax, click on the **VB Script Language Reference** link at the bottom of the **Edit Section Scripts** dialog. It is suggested that you bookmark the link in your Internet browser for future reference.

Adding sections for sorting and grouping

In the previous tasks, we worked with adding, formatting, and positioning fields in the detail section. Now we will work with the other default sections in the report template and will also add a section for sorting and grouping the information in the final report. For background information, a brief overview of the role of the sections is given. A default template has the following five sections:

- **Report Header**: Fields and labels in this section print once at the very beginning of the report. Used for a title page or summary.
- **Page Header**: Fields and labels in this section print once at the top of each page in the report. Typically used for a report name and identification of the user running the report.
- **Detail Section**: Fields and labels in this section print once for each record processed by the report. This is the workhorse part of the report template.
- **Page Footer**: Fields and labels in this section print once at the bottom of each page in the report. Mainly used for pagination.
- **Report Footer**: Fields and labels in this section print once at the very end of the report. Typically used for global totals related to the data processed.

You have the ability to add one or more custom section pairs to the report template. When you add a section both a header and a footer section are added. These added sections relate to and modify the detail section. Typical usages for these added sections are building sorts into the report, grouping the way the contacts are reported, and creating subtotals relative to the data in the detail section.

This task will introduce you to configuring and using the report sections. In addition to configuring the default header and footer section, we will add a custom section to sort and group the data in the report by city.

Getting ready

If you are doing this task immediately after finishing the previous task, you should still have the Report Training template open for editing. If so, skip to step 3. Otherwise start at step 1.

How to do it...

1. From any screen in the ACT! program, click on **Reports** in the navigation bar on the left-hand side of the screen.
2. In the list of report templates, right-click on the **Report Training** template and select **Edit Report**.
3. Click the **Edit** menu and select **Define Sections**.
4. In the **Define Sections** dialog, click the **Add** button.
5. In the **Select a Field to Group By** dialog, make sure the **Select a record** type is **Contact**.
6. In **Fields** select **City** and click the **OK** button.

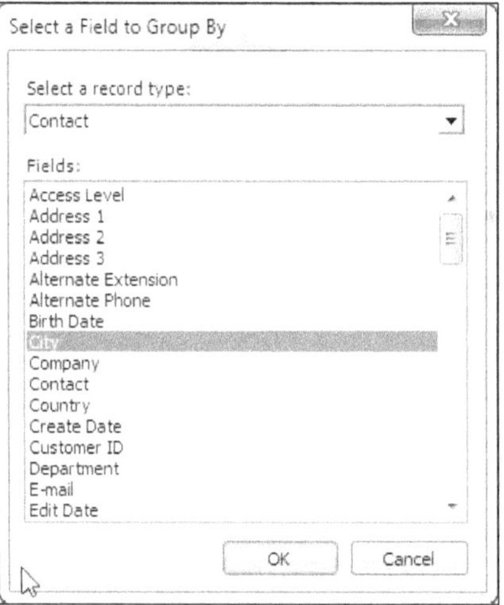

7. In the **Report Header** tree click on "**Section 1**.
8. For **Sorting**, click the dropdown and select **Ascending**.

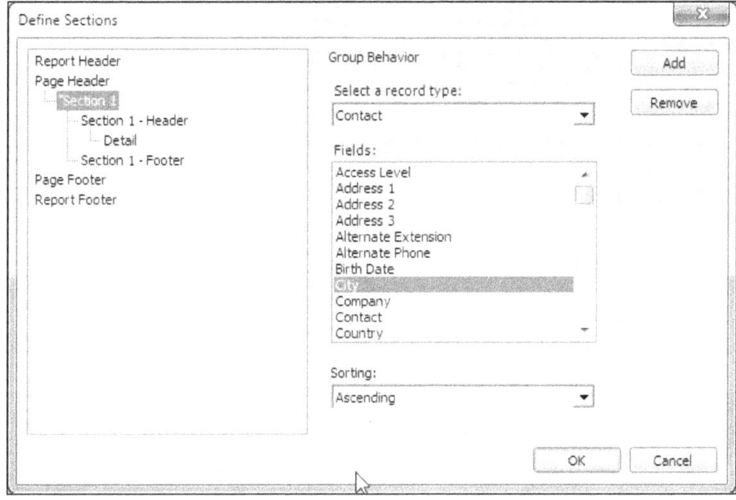

9. Click the **OK** button to add **Section1 - Header** and **Section1 - Footer** to the report template.
10. In the **Toolbox**, click on the **Text** tool.
11. In the **Report Header**, click and drag the crosshair pointer to create a box.
12. In **Properties**, **Layout** area set **Alignment** to **Center Middle**, **Height** to `1.0`, **Left** to `1.0`, **Top** to `0.1`, and **Width** to **6.0**.
13. In **Appearance**, **Text** property, type `Report Training`.
14. Set the **Font** to **36pt** and **style=Bold**.

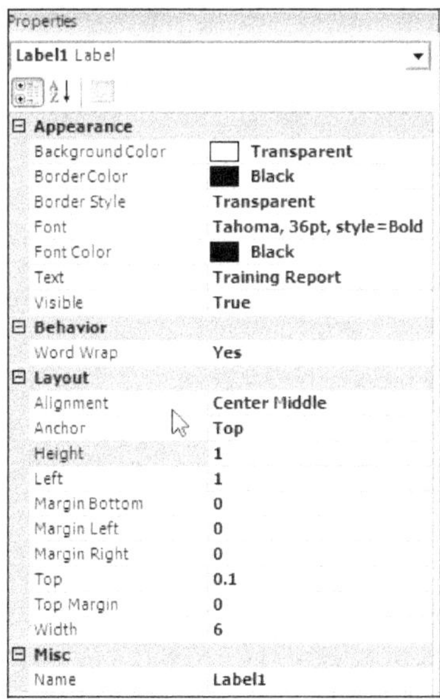

15. Click on the **Report Header** bar.
16. Set the **Force Page Break** property to **After**.
17. In the **Toolbox**, click on the **Text** tool.
18. In the **Page Header** click and drag the crosshair pointer to create a box.
19. In **Properties**, **Layout** area, set **Alignment** to **Center Middle**, **Height** to `0.4`, **Left** to `1.0`, **Top** to `0.05`, and **Width** to `3.0`.
20. In **Appearance**, **Text** property, type `Report Training`.
21. Set the **Font** to **20pt** and **style=Bold**.
22. In the **Toolbox**, click on the **Field** tool.
23. In the **Page Header** at about five-inches, click and drag the crosshair pointer down and to the right to create a box.
24. In the **Select Field** dialog, click the dropdown for **Select a record type** and choose **My Record**.
25. Uncheck **Include a label**.
26. In **Fields**, click on **Contact** and click the **Add** button.

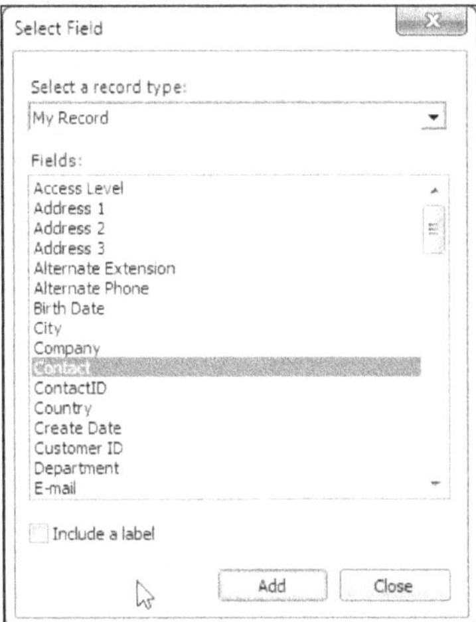

27. Click the **Close** button.
28. Click on the **My:Contact** field.
29. In **Properties**, **Misc area**, change the **Name** to **FContact2**.
30. In **Layout**, set alignment to **Left Middle**, **Height** to **0.2**, **Left** to **4.5**, **Top** to **0.2**, and **Width** to **2.5**.
31. Click on the **Page Header** bar.
32. Set the **Layout Property** to **0.5**.

33. In the **Toolbox**, click on the **System Field** tool.
34. In the **Page Footer**, click and drag the crosshair pointer to create a box.
35. In the **Select System Field** dialog, click on **Page Number**.
36. Uncheck **Include a label** and click the **Add** button.
37. Click the **Close** button.
38. Click on the **Page Number** field.
39. In **Properties**, **Layout** area, set **Alignment** to **Center Middle**, **Height** to `0.2`, **Left** to `3.5`, **Top** to `0.1`, and **Width** to `1.0`.
40. In the **Toolbox**, click on the **Rectangle** tool.
41. In the **Page Footer**, click and drag the crosshair pointer to create a box.
42. Click on the rectangular box created.
43. In **Properties**, **Layout** area set **Height** to `0.01`, **Left** to `0`, **Top** to `0`, and **Width** to `8.0`.
44. In **Appearance**, set the **Background Color** to **Black**.

45. In the **File** menu, select **Save** to save the template.

How it works...

With the number of steps involved, this task is very complex. Most of the steps involve operations that you did in previous tasks. The main thing introduced here was the use of custom sections to provide for grouping and sorting. The properties for the custom section control the field used for sorting and grouping. You are given four options for sorting, ascending, descending, and none.

A special note on grouping: If the field used for grouping is blank on any of the records, those records will make up a group and it will be the first group if the sort is ascending.

There's more...

When the custom section is being used for sorting only, the sort field doesn't need to be a field in the report. You can add multiple custom sections for sorting. The first section added is the primary sort, the second section added is the secondary sort, and so on.

Using sections for sub-totaling and totaling

In the previous task, we added a custom section to our training report template to group and sort the data by the content of the city field. Now let's assume that we would like to know how many records there were of each city included in the report. To do that, we will use another capability of the custom section, creating sub-totals and totals.

Getting ready

If you are doing this task immediately after finishing the previous task, you should still have the Report Training template open for editing. If so, skip to step 3. Otherwise start at step 1.

How to do it...

1. From any screen in the ACT! program, click on **Reports** in the navigation bar on the left-hand side of the screen.
2. In the list of report templates, right-click on the **Report Training** template and select **Edit Report**.
3. In the **Toolbox** click on the **Field** tool.
4. In the **Section 1 Header** at about one-inch from the left, click and drag the crosshair pointer down and to the right to create a box.

5. In the **Select Field** dialog click the dropdown for **Select a record type** and choose **Contact**.
6. In **Fields**, click on **City** and click the **Add** button.
7. Click the **Close** button.
8. Click on the **City** label and shift-click on the **C:City** field.
9. Right-click on either field, and select **Copy** from the menu.
10. Left-click on the **Section 1 - Footer** then right-click and select **Paste** from the menu.
11. Left-click on the **Report Footer** then right-click and select **Paste** from the menu.
12. In the **Section 1 - Header** click on the **City** label.
13. In the **Properties** panel, set **Word Wrap** to **No**, **Alignment** to **Left Middle**, **Height** to `0.17`, **Left** to `0.05`, **Top** to `0.02`, and **Width** to `0.5`.
14. Set the **Font** size to `10pt` and **Bold**.
15. In the **Section 1 Header** click on the **C:City** field.
16. In the **Properties** panel, set **Can Grow** to **No**, **Word Wrap** to **No**, **Alignment** to **Left Middle**, **Height** to `0.17`, Left to `0.6`, **Top** to `0.02`, and **Width** to `1.5`.
17. Set the **Font** size to `10pt` and **Regular**.
18. Click on the **Section 1 header** bar and set the **Height** property to `0.25`.
19. In the **Section 1 Footer** click on the **City** label.
20. In the **Properties** panel set **Word Wrap** to **No**, **Alignment** to **Left Middle**, **Height** to `0.17`, **Left** to `0.05`, **Top** to `0.02`, and **Width** to `0.75`.
21. Set the **Font** size to `10pt` and **Bold**.
22. In the **Text** property, type `City Count`.
23. In the **Section 1 - Footer**, click on the **C:City** field.
24. In the **Properties** panel, set **Can Grow** to **No**, **Word Wrap** to **No**, **Alignment** to **Right Middle**, **Height** to `0.17`, **Left** to `0.85`, **Top** to `0.02` and **Width** to `0.5`.
25. Set the **Font** size to `10pt` and **Regular**.
26. In the **Section 1 - Footer**, right-click on the **C:City** field and select **Properties** from the menu.
27. Click on the **Data** tab.

28. Click the **Summary** radio button.

29. Click on the **OK** button.
30. In the **Toolbox**, click on the **Rectangle** tool.
31. In the **Section 1** - **Footer**, click and drag the crosshair pointer to create a box.
32. Click on the rectangle box created.
33. In **Properties**, **Layout** area, set **Height** to `0.01`, **Left** to `0`, **Top** to `0.2`, and **Width** to `8.0`.
34. In **Appearance**, set the **Background Color** to **Black**.
35. Click on the **Section 1 Footer** bar and set the **Height** property to `0.25`.
36. In the **Report Footer**, click on the **City label**.
37. In the **Properties** panel, set **Word Wrap** to **No**, **Alignment** to **Left Middle**, **Height** to `0.17`, **Left** to `0.05`, **Top** to `0.2`, and **Width** to `0.85`.
38. Set the **Font** size to `10pt` and **Bold**.
39. In the **Text** property, type `Total Count`.
40. In the **Section 1 footer**, click on the **C:City** field.
41. In the **Properties** panel set **Can Grow** to **No**, **Word Wrap** to **No**, **Alignment** to **Right Middle**, **Height** to `0.17`, **Left** to `0.95`, **Top** to `0.2`, and **Width** to `0.5`.
42. Set the **Font** size to **10pt** and **Regular**.
43. In the **Report Footer**, right-click on the **C:City** field and select **Properties** from the menu.

44. Click on the **Data** tab.
45. Click the **Summary** radio button.
46. Click on the **OK** button.
47. In the **Toolbox**, click on the **Rectangle** tool.
48. In the **Report Footer** click and drag the crosshair pointer to create a box.
49. Click on the rectangle box created.
50. In **Properties**, **Layout** area set **Height** to `0.01`, **Left** to `0`, **Top** to `0`, and **Width** to `8.0`.
51. In **Appearance**, set the **Background Color** to **Black**.

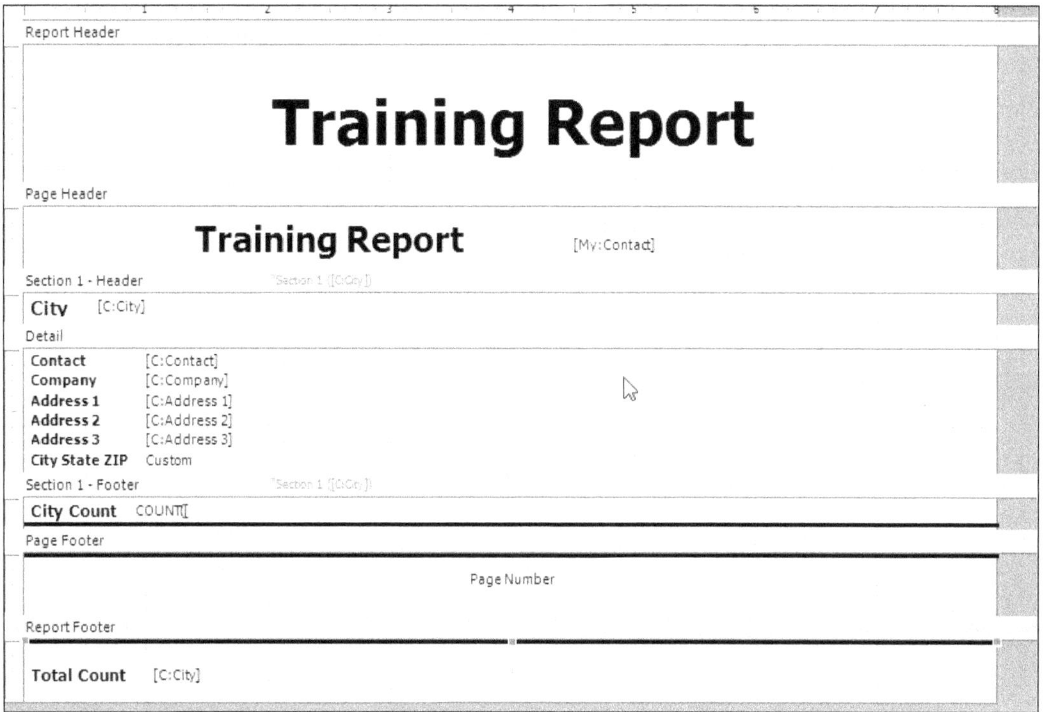

52. Click the **File** menu and select **Save**.

53. Click the **File** menu and select **Print Preview** to verify the report template.

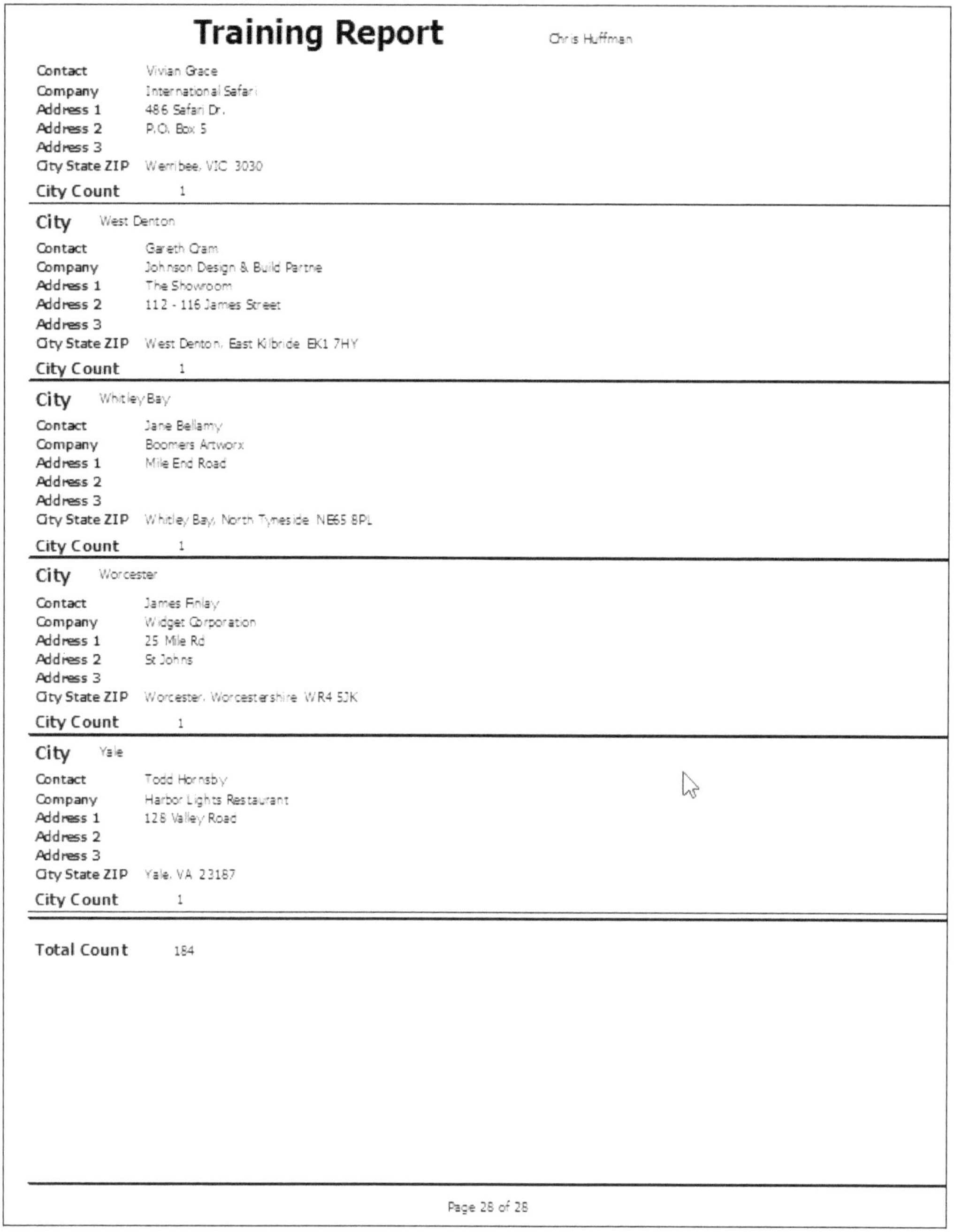

Training Report Chris Huffman

Contact Vivian Grace
Company International Safari
Address 1 486 Safari Dr.
Address 2 P.O. Box 5
Address 3
City State ZIP Werribee, VIC 3030
City Count 1

City West Denton
Contact Gareth Cram
Company Johnson Design & Build Partne
Address 1 The Showroom
Address 2 112 - 116 James Street
Address 3
City State ZIP West Denton, East Kilbride EK1 7HY
City Count 1

City Whitley Bay
Contact Jane Bellamy
Company Boomers Artworx
Address 1 Mile End Road
Address 2
Address 3
City State ZIP Whitley Bay, North Tyneside NE65 8PL
City Count 1

City Worcester
Contact James Finlay
Company Widget Corporation
Address 1 25 Mile Rd
Address 2 St Johns
Address 3
City State ZIP Worcester, Worcestershire WR4 5JK
City Count 1

City Yale
Contact Todd Hornsby
Company Harbor Lights Restaurant
Address 1 128 Valley Road
Address 2
Address 3
City State ZIP Yale, VA 23187
City Count 1

Total Count 184

Page 28 of 28

How it works...

As with the previous task, this task has a large number of steps. Most of the steps involved operations that you did in previous tasks. When working with individual fields as we were here, the steps can get very repetitive. Contrast this with an earlier task where we could select several similar report objects at the same time and set the preferences as a group.

Placement is very important for totaling. Note that a summary field placed in the custom section footer, gives a total for the range of the group defined by the section grouping. The same field with the same properties placed in the **Report Footer**, gives a global total for the entire report. Most fields can be set to do a count summary. When the field is numeric or currency, additional summary options are available.

There's more...

Keep in mind that when using the count summary, each record processed will be counted even if that field is blank.

5

Subreports and Scripting Techniques

In this chapter, we will cover:

- Formatting a List Type report
- Adding subreports to a report
- Adding fields to the secondary contacts subreport
- Adding fields to the history subreport
- Scripting basics by example
- Reverse engineering a set of complex scripts

Introduction

After reading this chapter you will be able to use more of the capabilities of the ACT! reports editor.

In this chapter, we continue to work with the ACT! report editor. In *Chapter 4, Working with the Report Editor*, we went through the tasks that are required to build a report template based on a single ACT! database table. Such single table reports are useful for making hard copies of database records. Another use for such reports is to create an electronic copy such as a PDF file of contact record data that can be sent via email to someone else. However, to make use of the database one-to-many relationships between the different database tables in a report, you need to use subreports.

A subreport is the equivalent of building another report within the main report template. While they are very similar in nature, there are differences to consider. The addition of subreports to a main report allows creation of more complex reports that involve more than one of the ACT! database tables. In fact, some of the ACT! tables such as Activities, History, Notes, and Secondary Contacts can only be accessed via a subreport. Sub reports can be added to any format report, form style or list style. The report template we created in *Chapter 4*, would be classed as a form style template. To demonstrate the formatting of a list style report, we will first convert our training report template into a list style report, before adding subreports.

The ACT! report editor also allows the embedding of Visual Basic programming scripts in report templates. In most cases, these scripts are program snippets that integrate with the underlying code of the report template. *Chapter 4* included a simple programming script to concatenate multiple fields into one custom field. Here we will look at a couple of more complex program scripts that involve conditional situations. Finally we will dissect the scripts in a template with very complex scripts.

Formatting a List Type report

Converting the training report into a list style report mainly involves rearranging the fields and labels. However field size (width) becomes very important so that line space is appropriately used.

Getting ready

If you are doing this task immediately after finishing the last task in *Chapter 4*, you should still have the Report Training template open for editing. If so, skip to step 3. Otherwise start at step 1.

How to do it...

1. From any screen in the ACT! program, click on **Reports** in the navigation bar on the left-hand side of the screen.
2. In the list of report templates, right-click on the **Report Training** template and select **Edit Report**.
3. Click the **File** menu and select **Save As...**.
4. For a **File Name**, type `Report Training 2.rep`.
5. Click the **Save** button to save the report.
6. In the **Report Header** section, click on the **Training Report** title.
7. In the **Properties** panel, **Text** property, add the number `2` to the title.
8. In the **Page Header** section, click on the **Training Report** title.
9. In the **Properties** panel, **Text** property, add the number `2` to the title.

10. In the **Section 1 Header**, delete the **C:City** field and title.

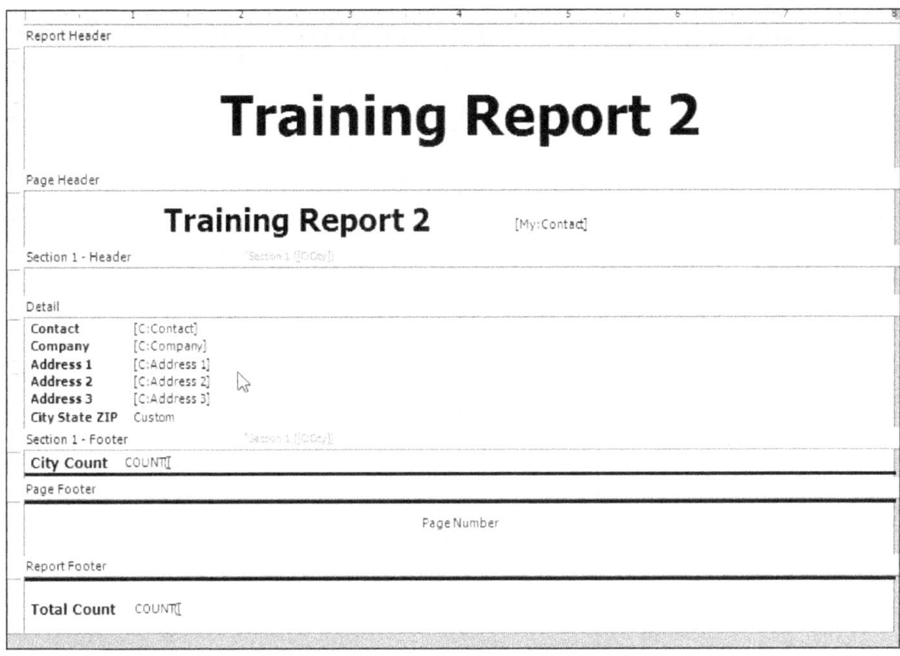

11. One at a time, drag the field labels from the **Detail** section to the **Section 1** header and arrange them across the work space as shown in the screenshot:

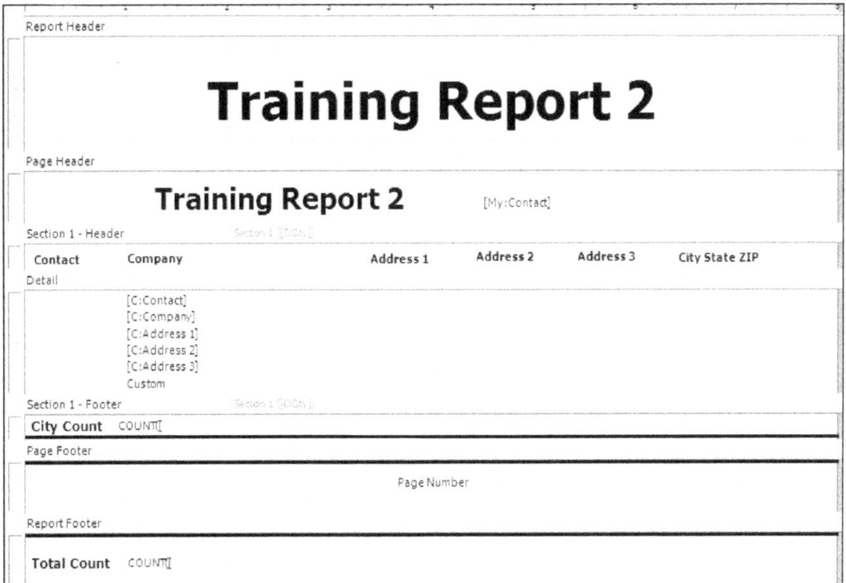

12. Click on the **C:Contact** field and then hold the *Shift* key and click on each of the **C:Compnay**, **C:Address1**, **C:Address2**, **C:Address3**, and **Custom** fields.
13. In the **Properties** panel set the **Width** property to `1.0`.
14. One at a time, drag the fields in the **Detail** section so they remain in the **Detail** section but are positioned under the appropriate label as shown in the following screenshot:

15. In the **Toolbox** panel, click on the **Field** tool.
16. Position the field cross hair in the **Detail** section at about one and a half inches from the left-hand side and click and drag down and to the right to create a box about one-inch long.
17. In the **Select Field** dialog, make sure **Select a record type** is set to **Contact** and then double-click on the **Phone** field.
18. Click the **Close** button.
19. Click on the **Phone** label and set the following properties: **Font** to **Bold**, **Word Wrap** to **No**, **Alignment** to **Left Middle**, **Height** to `0.14`, **Left** to `1.0`, and **Width** to `1.0`.
20. Click on the **C:Phone** field and set the following properties: **Can Grow** to **N**o, **Word Wrap** to **No**, **Alignment** to **Left Middle**, **Height** to `0.14`, **Left** to `2.5`, **Width** to `1.0`, and **Name** to `FPhone1`.

21. Click on the **Phone** label and drag it from the **Detail** section to the **Section 1** header and position it between the **Company** and the **Address 1** labels.

22. Drag the **C:Phone** field to a position between the **C:Company** and the **C:Address 1** fields.

23. Place the cursor in the left margin of the template workspace. The cursor will change to a dark arrow. Point the arrow at the labels in **Section 1 Header** and left-click to select all the labels as shown in the following screenshot:

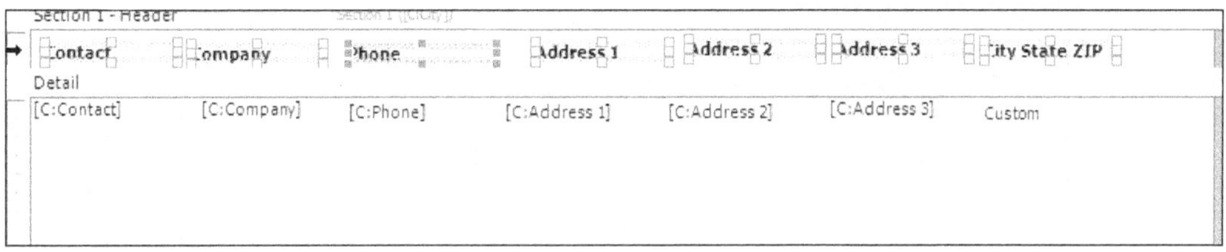

24. Set the **Top** property to `0.1`.

25. Place the cursor in the left margin of the template workspace. Point the arrow at the fields in **Detail** section. Left-click to select all the fields. If necessary, click and drag the cursor up or down to make sure all the fields are selected.

26. Set the **Top** property to `0.05`.

27. Click on the **C:Contact** field and then while holding down the *Shift* key, click on the **Contact** label. Set the **Left** property to `0.05` and **Width** to `1.25`.

28. Click on the **C:Company** field and then while holding down the *Shift* key, click on the **Company** label. Set the **Left** property to `1.35` and **Width** to `1.25`.

29. Click on the **C:Phone** field and then while holding down the *Shift* key, click on the **Phone** label. Set the **Left** property to `2.65` and **Width** to `0.75`.

30. Click on the **C:Address1** field and then while holding down the *Shift* key, click on the **Address1** label. Set the **Left** property to `3.45` and **Width** to `1.25`.

31. Click on the **C:Address2** field and then while holding down the *Shift* key, click on the **Address2** label. Set the **Left** property to `4.75` and **Width** to `1.0`.

32. Click on the **C:Address3** field and then while holding down the *Shift* key, click on the **Address3** label. Set the **Left** property to `5.8` and **Width** to `0.75`.

33. Click on the **Custom** field and then while holding down the *Shift* key, click on the **City State ZIP** label. Set the **Left** property to `6.6` and **Width** to `1.35`.

34. In the **Toolbox** click on the **Rectangle** tool.

35. In the **Detail section**, click and drag the crosshair pointer to create a box.

36. Click on the rectangular box created.

37. In **Properties**, set **Height** to `0.01`, **Left** to `0`, **Top** to `0`, **Width** to `8.0` and **Background Color** to **Black**.

38. Click the **File** menu and select **Save**.

How it works...

In this task, we first preserved our original report template by doing a **Save As** to create a second report. This is a good practice when you're making significant changes to a template. Most of the steps here are similar to actions preformed in *Chapter 4*. The naming field for **Section 1** was deleted but the sorting and grouping wasn't, so the section totals and the global total at the end are still valid. Most of the steps in this task involved moving the existing fields and field labels into new positions. The phone field was added to the name and addresses fields of the original report. I introduced a new technique for selecting multiple template objects by using the cursor in the left margin of the workspace. This can be a real time saver when working with the fields in a list style report.

The main challenge is the sizing and the placement of the fields and fields labels. In *Chapter 4*, the filed placement used a uniform field height and line spacing so the vertical placement was fairly simple. Here the considerations are how much width is required to accommodate the field data. Let us use `0.05` inches. The field widths we used here are somewhat arbitrary based on my past experience. It's better to test the sizes with the report preview and adjust according. Another option is to turn on the **Can Grow** and **Word Wrap** for selected fields. Also note that we are able to select both the field label and the field itself at the same time even though they are located in different sections and set the size and location properties for both at the same time.

There's more...

In a list style report template, consideration needs to be given to placement of the field labels. As a general rule there are three choices: at the top of the Detail section, an added section header, or the Page Header. The placement chosen must consider when the field labels would be repeated.

If placed in the Detail section, they would repeat for every record processed by the Detail section as this would make the final report very cluttered and seldom used.

If placed in an added section header as in our training report, the field labels would repeat every time there was a break to a new group. When the detail section is complex, this may be the desirable location.

If place in the Page Header, the field labels will repeat at the top of each page. When there aren't any added sections or the contact processed for each section group, this would be the preferred location for the field labels.

Adding subreports to a report

You can add one or more subreports to a main report. While the subreport is added in the main report, at that point the subreport is undefined. Typically you add a name that indicates the purpose of the subreport. The subreport becomes defined by the table used to add field to the subreport.

Getting ready

If you are doing this task immediately after finishing the previous task, you should still have the Report Training 2 template open for editing. If so, skip to step 3. Otherwise start at step 1.

How to do it...

1. From any screen in the ACT! program, click on **Reports** in the navigation bar on the left-hand side of the screen.
2. In the list of report templates right-click on the **Report Training 2** template and select **Edit Report**.
3. In the **Toolbox**, click on **Subreport**.
4. Place the crosshair cursor in the left margin of the template workspace. Point it below the row of field objects in the **Detail** section. Click and drag down about 1/4 inch. Release the left mouse button.
5. In the **Subreports** dialog, set the **Subreport name** to Secondary Contacts.
6. Select **FContactID1** as the link field.

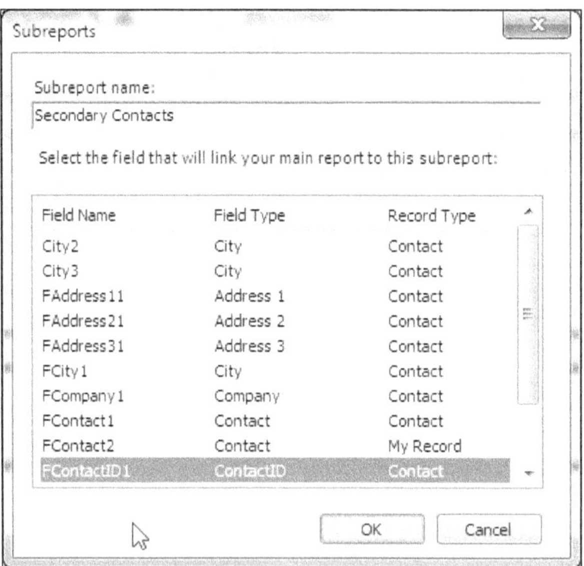

7. Click the **OK** button.
8. Click on the subreport.
9. In **Properties**, set **Height** to `0.2`, **Top** to `0.3`, and **Width** to `8.0`.
10. In the **Toolbox**, click on **Subreport**.
11. Place the crosshair cursor in the left margin of the template workspace. Point it below the subreport previously inserted. Click and drag down about 1/4 inch. Release the left mouse button.
12. In the **Subreports** dialog, set the **Subreport name** to `History`.
13. Select **FContactID1** as the link field.

14. Click the **OK** button.
15. Click on the subreport.
16. In **Properties**, set **Height** to `0.2`, **Top** to `0.6`, and **Width** to `8.0`.

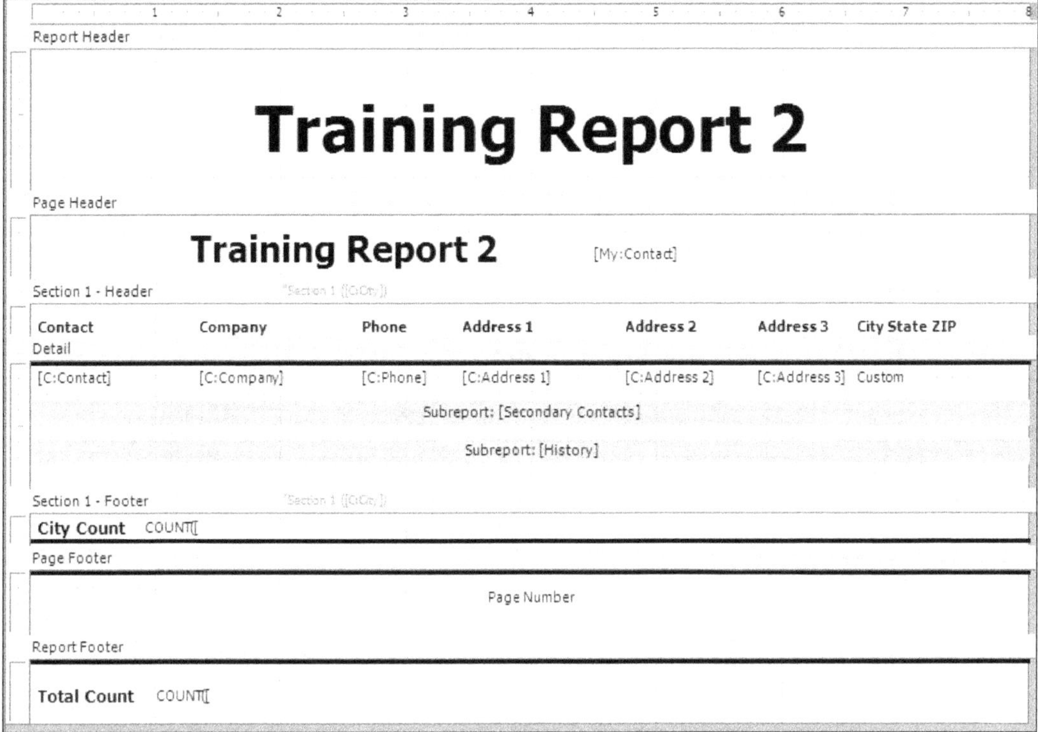

17. Click on the **Detail** section bar.
18. Set the **Height** property to `0.9` and **HideOnEmptySubreport** to **No**.
19. Click the **File** menu and select **Save**.

How it works...

At this point, we have attached two subreports to the main report. We decided that one of the subreports will be to report the secondary contacts for each contact record processed. The other subreport will be for Histories attached to each contact record processed.

Note that we used the **FCotactID** field to link each subreport to the main report. If you remember, that was a field that we added in *Chapter 4* and then hid in the main report. The Contact ID is a unique number that is assigned to each record when the contact is first added to the database. We use that field as the link field rather than the contact name because of its unique nature. If we were to use the contact name and we had two contacts with the same name (for example John Smith), the report wouldn't know which secondary contacts or histories belonged to which John Smith.

The height that the subreport is set to is arbitrary. I used 0.2 inches so the name would be visible but I could make it any height so long as it's at least 0.01. The Can Grow property set to Yes will allow it to expand to accommodate the data reported in the subreport.

The HideOnEmprySubreport property set to Yes will cause the contact in the main report to be filtered out as there isn't any data in the subreport. In some cases, that is desirable but for our purposes we set it to No so that all contact records will print.

Adding fields to the secondary contacts subreport

Now that we've added two subreports to the main template body; we need to add the appropriate fields to the subreport and format the subreport. This process is similar to the tasks we performed in *Chapter 4*, however there are some things that are unique to subreports. The first subreport we'll configure is the one we named Secondary Contacts.

Getting ready

If you are doing this task immediately after finishing your previous task, you should still have the Report Training 2 template open for editing. If so, skip to step 3. Otherwise start at step 1.

How to do it...

1. From any screen in the ACT! program, click on **Reports** in the navigation bar on the left-hand side of the screen.
2. In the list of report templates, right-click on the **Report Training 2** template and select **Edit Report**.
3. In the field immediately above the **Toolbox**, click the dropdown and select **Secondary Contacts**.

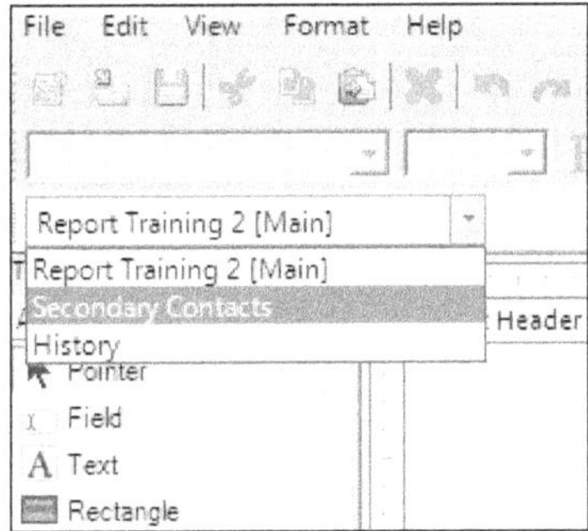

4. Click on the **Header** bar and set the properties **Visible** to **Yes** and **Height** to `0.5`.
5. Click on the **Detail** bar and set the properties **Visible** to **Yes** and **Height** to `0.5`.
6. At the top of the **Properties** panel, click the dropdown and select **Secondary Contacts Report**.
7. Set the **Margin Left** to `0.25`, the **Margin Right** to `0.25`, and the **Font** to **Tahoma regular** `8` point.
8. In the **Toolbox** panel, click on the **Field** tool.
9. Position the cross hair cursor in the **Detail** section at about one and a half inches from the left-hand side and click and drag down and right to create a box about one-inch long.
10. In the **Select Field** dialog, make sure **Select a record type** is set to **Secondary Contact** and then double-click on the following fields:
    - **Contact**
    - **Company**
    - **Phone**

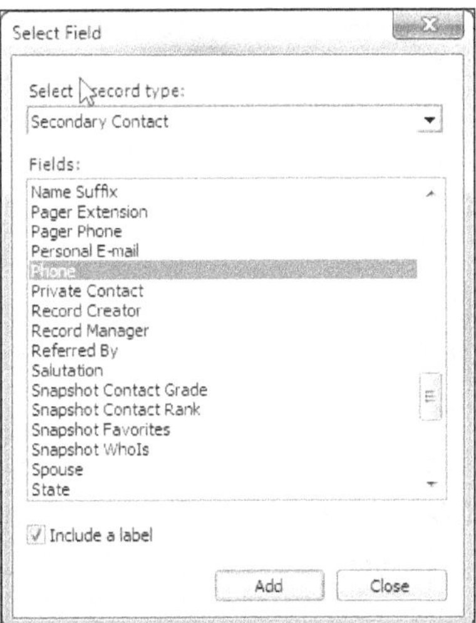

11. Click the **Close** button.
12. Drag the **Contact**, **Company**, and **Phone** labels into the **Header** section and position similar, as shown in the following screenshot:

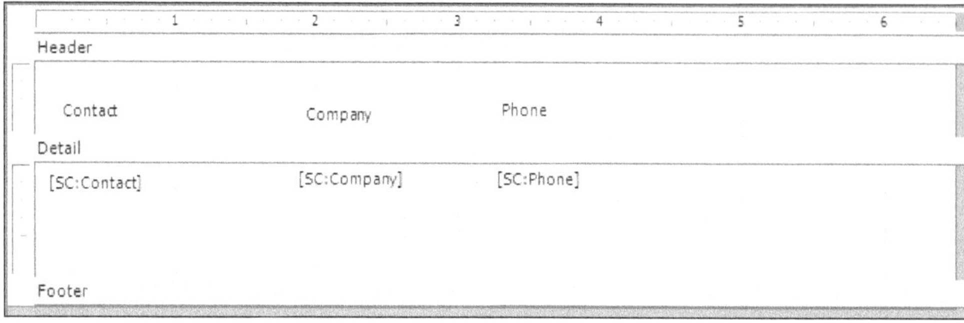

13. Drag the **SC:Contact**, **SC:Company**, and **SC:Phone** to positions similar to the way shown in the screenshot.
14. In the **Toolbox** panel, click on the **Text** tool.
15. Position the cross hair cursor in the **Header** section near the upper left corner and click and drag down and to the right to create a box about 1-inch long.
16. Click on the text field created and set the properties as follows:
    - **Background color**: **Black**
    - **Font color**: **White**
    - **Font Style**: **Bold**
    - **Text**: **Secondary Contacts**
    - **Word Wrap**: **No**
    - **Alignment**: **Left Middle**
    - **Height**: `0.15`
    - **Left**: `0`
    - **Top**: `0`
    - **Width**: `1.25`
17. Place the cursor in the left margin of the template workspace so that the arrow points to the field labels in the **Header** section. Click to select the field labels. Set the properties as follows:
    - **Font**: **Bold Underline**
    - **Word Wrap**: **No**
    - **Alignment**: **Left Middle**

- **Height**: `0.15`
- **Top**: `0.2`
- **Width**: `1.0`

18. Place the cursor in the left margin of the template workspace so that the arrow points to the **SC:fields** in the **Detail** section. Click to select the fields. Set the properties as follows:
    - **Can Grow**: **No**
    - **Word Wrap**: **No**
    - **Alignment**: **Left Middle**
    - **Height**: `0.15`
    - **Top**: `0.02`
    - **Width**: `1.25`
19. Click on the **Contact** label and then while holding down the *Shift* key, click on the **SC:Contact** field. Set the **Left** property to `0.05`.
20. Click on the **Company** label and then while holding down the *Shift* key, click on the **SC:Company** field. Set the **Left** property to `1.35`.
21. Click on the **Phone** label and then while holding down the *Shift* key, click on the **SC: Phone** field. Set the **Left** property to `1.65`.
22. In the **Toolbox**, click on the **Rectangle** tool.
23. Point the crosshair cursor in the open area of the **Detail** section and click and drag to draw a box about 1.0 inch long.
24. Click on the Rectangular box and set the properties as follows:
    - **Background Color**: **Black**
    - **Height**: `0.01`
    - **Top**: `0.0`
    - **Left**: `0.0`
    - **Width**: `3.5`
25. Click the **Header** bar and set the **Height** property to `0.35`.
26. Click the **Detail** bar and set the **Height** property to `0.25`.
27. Right-click on the rectangle in the **Detail** section and select **Copy**.
28. Left-click on the **Footer** bar and then right-click and select **Paste**.

29. Click on the **Footer** bar and set the **Visible** property to **Yes**.

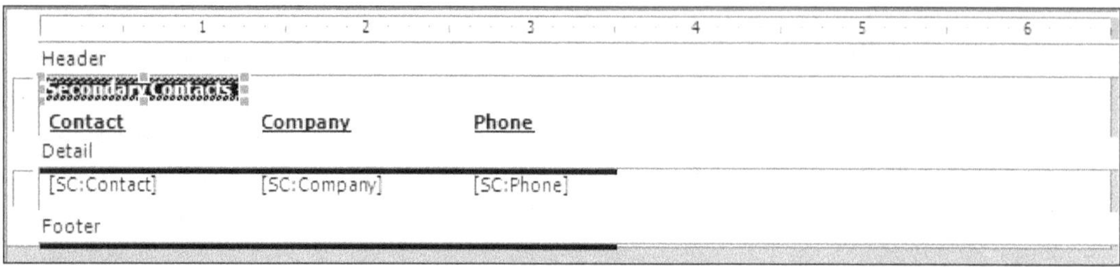

30. In the field immediately above the **Toolbox**, click the dropdown and select **Report Training 2 (Main)**.
31. Click the **File** menu and select **Save**.

How it works...

The addition and formatting of the fields added to the subreport is very similar to adding fields to the main report. The differences include that all the sections of the subreport default to not visible. There isn't any page header or footer and the report header and footer are simply called header and footer. In most cases, you will want to add a text field to identify the subreport as we did with Secondary Contacts field and used reversed text to make the title stand out.

Because part of my goal is to show techniques to help designing report templates, I used a number of shortcuts for selecting and setting properties that weren't used in *Chapter 4*. Also note that I didn't change the default field objects names. The subreport report objects are separate from the main report objects and with only a few field objects involved, renaming them to group them in the list is optional.

Adding fields to the history subreport

In the previous task, we added a limited number of fields to the subreport and didn't add any custom sections for grouping or sorting. In this task we will be adding more fields and making use of sorting and grouping.

Getting ready

If you are doing this task immediately after finishing the previous task, you should still have the Report Training 2 template open for editing. If so, skip to step 3. Otherwise start at step 1.

How to do it...

1. From any screen in the ACT! program, click on **Reports** in the navigation bar on the left-hand side of the screen.
2. In the list of report templates, right-click on the **Report Training 2** template and select **Edit Report**.
3. In the field immediately above the **Toolbox**, click the dropdown and select **History**.
4. Click on the **Header** bar and set the properties **Visible** to **Yes** and **Height** to `0.5`.
5. Click on the **Detail** bar and set the properties **Visible** to **Yes** and **Height** to `0.5`.
6. At the top of the **Properties** panel, click the dropdown and select **History Report**.
7. Set the **Margin Left** to `0.25`, the **Margin Right** to `0.25`, and the **Font** to **Tahoma regular** `8` point.
8. In the **Toolbox** panel, click on the **Field** tool.
9. Position the cross hair cursor in the **Detail** section at about one and a half inches from the left side and click and drag down and right to create a box about one-inch long.
10. In the **Select Field** dialog, make sure **Select a record type** is set to **Contact History** and then double-click on the following fields:
    - **Date**
    - **Result**
    - **Regarding**
    - **Details**

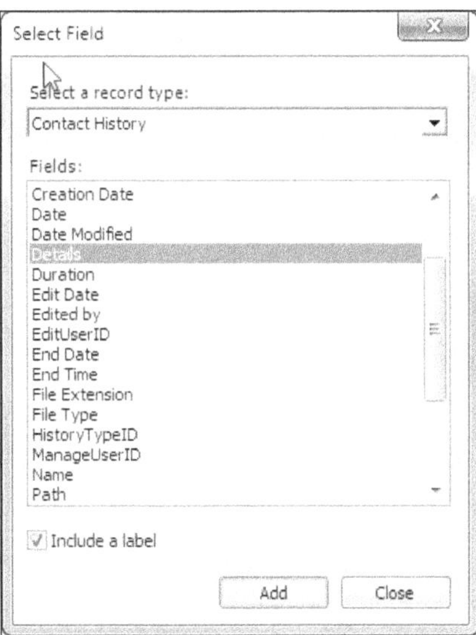

11. Click the **Close** button.
12. Drag the **Date**, **Result**, **Regarding**, and **Details** labels into the **Header** section and position similar to the way shown in the following screenshot:

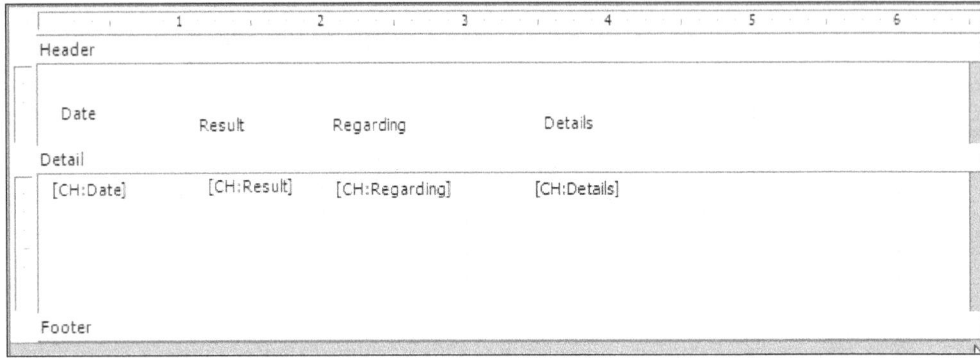

13. Drag the **CH:Date**, **CH:Result**, **CH:Regarding**, and **CH:Details** to positions similar to the way shown in the screenshot.
14. In the **Toolbox** panel, click on the **Text** tool.
15. Position the cross hair cursor in the **Header** section at about near the upper left corner and click and drag down and to the right to create a box about one-inch long.
16. Click on the text field created and set the properties as follows
    - **Background color**: **Black**
    - **Font Color**: **White**
    - **Font Style**: **Bold**
    - **Text** : **Secondary Contacts**
    - **Word Wrap**: **No**
    - **Alignment**: **Left Middle**
    - **Height**: `0.15`
    - **Left**: `0`
    - **Top**: `0`
    - **Width**: `0.5`
17. Place the cursor in the left margin of the template workspace so that the arrow points to the field labels in the **Header** section. Click to select the field labels. Set the properties as follows:
    - **Font**: **Bold Underline**
    - **Word Wrap**: **No**
    - **Alignment**: **Left Middle**

- **Height**: `0.15`
- **Top**: `0.2`
- **Width**: `0.95`

18. Right-click on the **CH:Date** field and select **Properties**.
19. In **the Field Properties** dialog, click on the **Format** tab and then select **M/d/yyyy**.

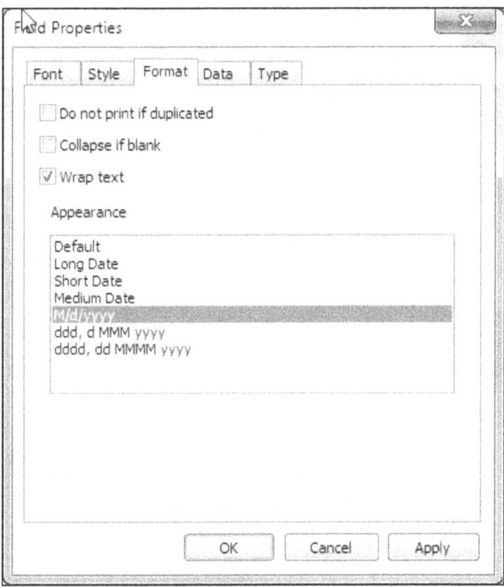

20. Click the **OK** button.
21. Place the cursor in the left margin of the template workspace so that the arrow points to the **CH:fields** in the **Detail** section. Click to select the fields. Set the properties as follows:
    - **Can Grow**: **Yes**
    - **Word Wrap**: **Yes**
    - **Alignment**: **Left Middle**
    - **Height**: `0.15`
    - **Top**: `0.02`
    - **Width**: `0.95`
22. Click on the **Date** label and then while holding down the *Shift* key, click on the **CH:Date** field. Set the **Left** property to `0.05`.
23. Click on the **Result** label and while holding down the *Shift* key, click on the **CH:Result** field. Set the **Left** property to `1.05`.

24. Click on the **Regarding** label and then while holding down the *Shift* key, click on the **CH:Regarding** field. Set the **Left** property to `2.05` and the **Width** to `1.45`.
25. Click on the **Details** label and then while holding down the *Shift* key, click on the **CH: Details** field. Set the **Left** property to `3.55` and the **Width** to `4.4`.
26. In the **Toolbox**, click on the **Rectangle** tool.
27. Point the crosshair cursor in the open area of the **Detail** section and click and drag to draw a box about 1.0 inch long.
28. Click on the Rectangular box and set the properties as follows:
    - **Background Color**: **Black**
    - **Height**: `0.01`
    - **Top**: `0.0`
    - **Left**: `0.0`
    - **Width**: `8.0`
29. Click the **Header** bar and set the **Height** property to `0.35`.
30. Click the **Detail** bar and set the **Height** property to `0.25`.
31. Right-click on the rectangle in the **Detail** section and select **Copy**.
32. Left-click on the **Footer** bar and then right-click and select **Paste**.
33. Click on the **Footer** bar and set the **Visible** property to **Yes**.

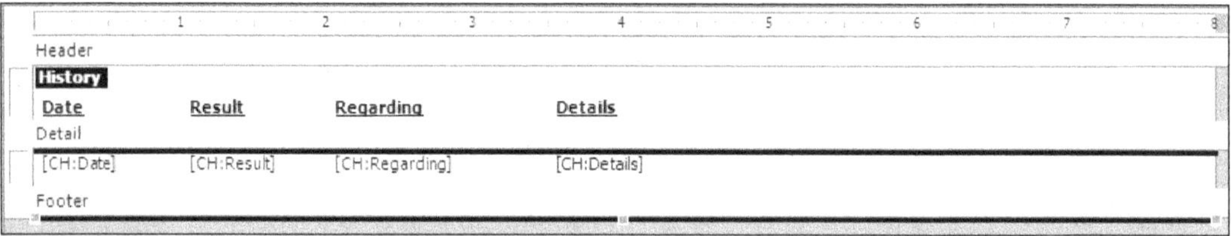

34. Double-click on the **Detail** bar.
35. In the **Define Sections** dialog, click on the **Add** button.
36. In the **Select a Field to Group By** dialog, make sure **Select a record type** is set to **Contact History** and then click on **Results**.
37. Click the **OK** button.

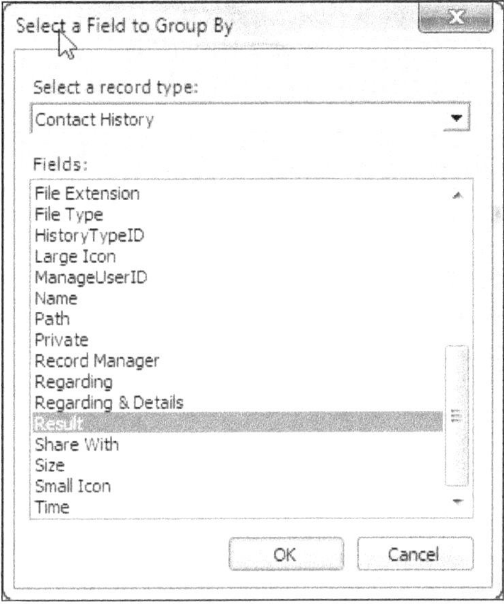

38. In the **Define Sections** dialog click on the **Add** button.
39. In the **Select a Field to Group By** dialog, make sure **Select a record type** is set to **Contact History** and then click on **Date**.
40. Click the **OK** button.

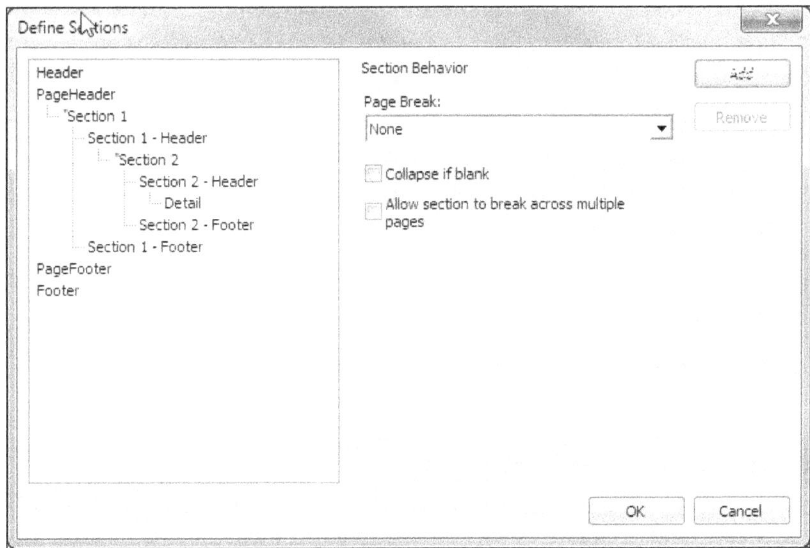

41. Click the **OK** button to close the **Define Sections** dialog.

42. In turn, click on the **Section 1 Header**, **Section 2 Header**, **Section 1 Footer**, and **Section 2 Footer** and set the **Height** property to `0.0`.
43. In the field immediately above the **Toolbox**, click the dropdown and select **Report Training 2 (Main)**.
44. Click the **File** menu and select **Save**.

How it works...

Most of the configuring of the **History** subreport was the same as the **Secondary Contacts** subreports. The **Secondary Contacts** subreport was a simple listing report and all the fields were set to not have word wrap and not be able to grow. In the **History** subreport, several of the fields have the potential of requiring more than one line to show all the field data so the fields are set to allow word wrap and are able to grow to accommodate the additional lines. This could be done selectively to allow some fields to word wrap and grow and others to be of fixed height even if the data exceeded field size.

A special note about the **Details** field. In the database, the field is coded for **Rich Text Format** (**RTF**). This causes trouble for reports. There is property for RTF that determines if the field in the report interprets the RTF coding. When set to interpret, the RTF coding the font size set for the field in the template has no meaning and the RTF coding will control things such as font type, style, and size. Unfortunately turning off the RTF property isn't an answer. While the font for the field will now be used for the data, it doesn't strip out the RTF coding and it clutters the data. Neither answer is good.

When you use a date field in an ACT! Report you need to know that all date fields in the database include a time element. In the case of the date field here, we didn't want the time component so we had to set the field properties to format the date without the time component.

We also added two custom sections for sorting purposes to the subreport. The primary sort will be by the history results (Call Completed, Meeting Held, and so on). Within each result group, the history events will be sorted by date.

See also

Totaling was not included in the subreports but it can be done the same way as was shown in Chapter 4.

Scripting basics by example

The ACT! Report capabilities can be dramatically expanded through the use of embedded Visual Basic program scripts. The example we will use here is relatively simple but does demand a working knowledge of Visual Basic. It uses a series of conditional statements to assemble the contact's name complete with any prefixes and suffixes.

Getting ready

Because the particular script example we will be creating would most often be used in an envelope or label template, we will build our script in a new, empty envelope template.

How to do it...

1. From any screen in the ACT! program, click on **Reports** in the navigation bar on the left side of the screen.
2. Click on **New Report Template**.
3. In the **New Report** dialog, double click on **Contact Envelopes**.
4. In the **New Envelope** dialog, select **Envelope #10** in the **Select an envelope size** field and then click the **OK** button.

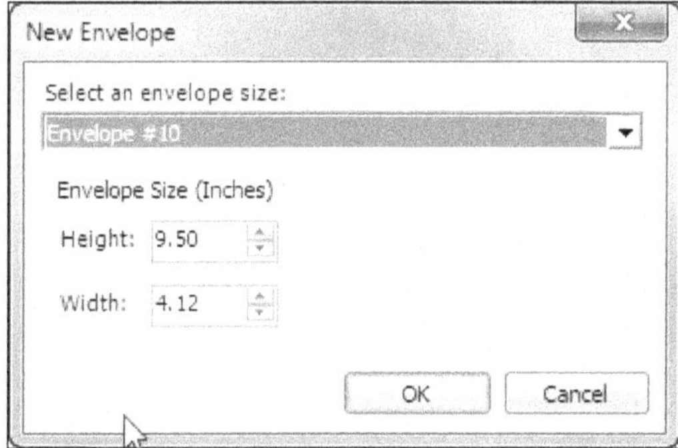

5. Click the **File** menu and select **Save As** and save the template as `Envelope Script Training`.
6. At the top of the **Properties** panel, click the dropdown and select **Envelope Script Training Report**.
7. Set the **Font** to **Tahoma**, **Regular**, and `12` Point.
8. In the **Toolbox** panel, click on the **Field** tool.
9. Position the cross hair cursor in the **Detail** section at about one and a half inches from the left-hand side and click and drag down and right to create a box about one-inch long.
10. In the **Select Field** dialog, make sure the **Select a record type** is set to **Contact**, uncheck the **Include a label** and then double-click on the following fields:
    - **Name Prefix**
    - **First Name**
    - **Last Name**
    - **Name Suffix**

11. Click the **Close** button.

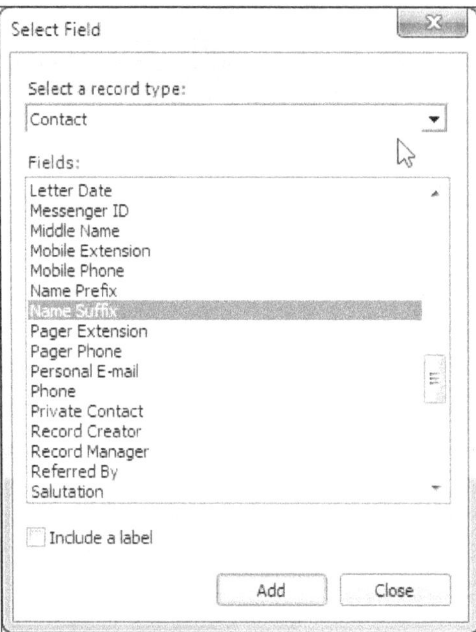

12. Click on the **C:Name Prefix** field and set the properties as follows:
    - **Can Grow**: **No**
    - **Word Wrap**: **No**
    - **Name** to `FNamePrefix1`
13. Click on the **C:First Name** field and set the properties as follows:
    - **Can Grow**: **No**
    - **Word Wrap**: **No**
14. Click on the **C:Last Name** field and set the properties as follows:
    - **Can Grow**: **No**
    - **Word Wrap**: **No**
    - **Name** to `FLastName1`
15. Click on the **C:Name Suffix** field and set the properties as follows:
    - **Can Grow**: **No**
    - **Word Wrap**: **No**
    - **Name** to `FNameSuffix1`

These four fields will be hidden later. For now, they can be used to verify that the script is working correctly.

16. In the **Toolbox** panel, click on the **System Field** tool.
17. Position the cross hair cursor in the **Detail** section at about one and a half inches from the top and four-inches from the left-hand side and click and drag down and to the right to create a box about three-inch long.
18. In the **Select System Field** dialog, uncheck **Include a label** and double-click on **Custom**. Click the **Close** button.

19. Click on the **Custom** field and set the properties as follows:
    - **Alignment**: **Left Middle**
    - **Height**: `0.2`
    - **Left**: `4.0`
    - **Top**: `1.5`
    - **Width**: `3.0`
    - **Name**: `CustomName1`
20. Right-click in the blank area below the envelope workspace and select **Edit Report Scripts**.
21. In the **Edit Report Scripts** use the dropdown to select **OnOpen**.

22. In the main area type the following code line:

    ```
    CustomName1.text = ""
    ```

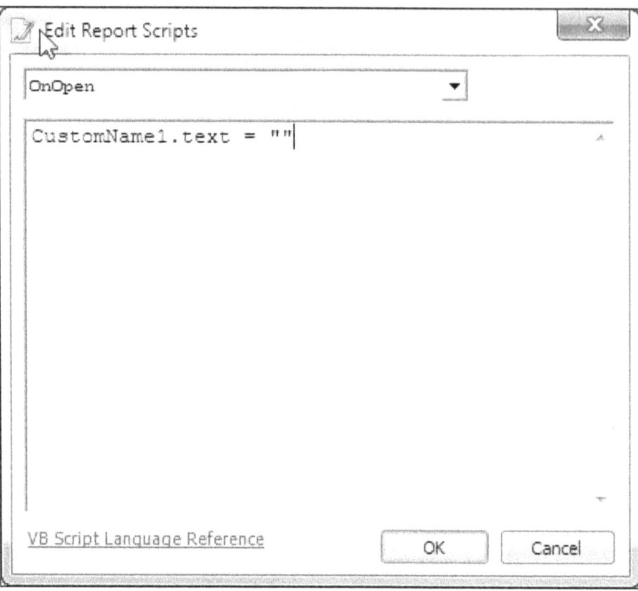

23. In the **Edit Report Scripts**, use the dropdown to select **OnClose**.
24. In the main area type the following code line:

    ```
    CustomName1.text = ""
    ```

25. Click the **OK** button.
26. Left-click on the **Detail** bar and then right-click and select **Edit Report Scripts**.
27. In the **Edit Section Scripts**: **OnPrint**, type the following code:

    ```
    CustomName1.Text = ""

    If FNamePrefix1 = Null Then

    Else
        CustomName1.Text = FNamePrefix1
    EndIf

    If FirstName1 = Null Then

    Else
        CustomName1.Text = CustomName1.Text&" "&FirstName1
    ```

```
EndIf
If FLastName1 = Null Then

Else
    CustomName1.Text = CustomName1.Text&" "&FLastName1
EndIf

If FNameSuffix1 = Null Then

Else
    CustomName1.Text = CustomName1.Text&" "&FNameSuffix1
EndIf
```

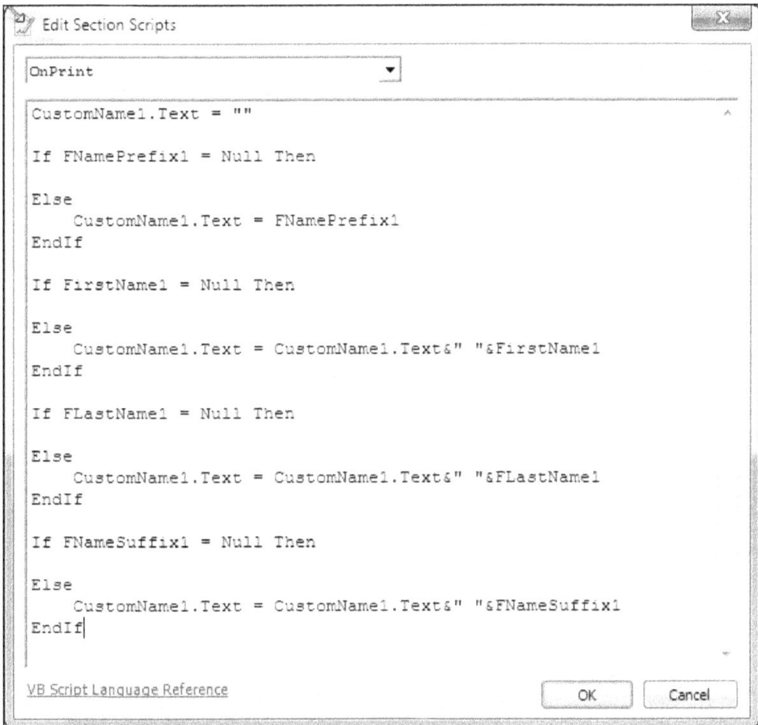

28. Click the **OK** button.

Coding tip: The ACT! report script editor doesn't have any text formatting tools. We should typically use WordPad to do our script coding and then copy the finished script into the **Edit Section Scripts** dialog.

29. Click the **File** menu and select **Print Preview** and verify the script program is working properly.

The ACT! report scripting doesn't provide any debugger. If a script doesn't work you will need to do visual debugging. Remember, a single misplaced or wrong character can cause a script to fail.

30. Click on the **C:Name Prefix** field and set the properties as follows:
    - **Visible**: **False**
    - **Height**: `0.01`
    - **Left**: `9.0`
    - **Top**: `0.01`
    - **Width**: `0.2`
31. Click on the **C:First Name** field and set the properties as follows:
    - **Visible**: **False**
    - **Height**: `0.01`
    - **Left**: `9.0`
    - **Top**: `0.03`
    - **Width**: `0.2`
32. Click on the **C:Last Name** field and set the properties as follows:
    - **Visible**: **False**
    - **Height**: `0.01`
    - **Left**: `9.0`
    - **Top**: `0.05`
    - **Width**: `0.2`

33. Click on the **C:Name Suffix** field and set the properties as follows:
    - **Visible**: **False**
    - **Height**: `0.01`
    - **Left**: `9.0`
    - **Top**: `0.07`
    - **Width**: `0.2`
34. Click the **File** menu and select **Save**.

How it works...

Constructing working program scripts involves several different functions. The first is adding the necessary fields to the report template. Because these fields will eventually be hidden, they can be added to any part of the workspace that isn't being other wise used at that time. The next thing to do is one or more custom fields as needed to receive data for display from the scripts.

The next thing to do is initialize the custom fields. This is done in the OnOpen dialog in the overall report script. If your script needs temporary variables that aren't intended for display, they should also be initialized in the OnOpen dialog. Though not necessary, it's a good practice to clear the custom fields and variables in the OnClose dialog.

Now, we're ready to code the actual working script. Because this script applies to the detail section, we need to open the Edit Section Script dialog for that section. Because this script applies to the report printing, we'll do the coding in the OnPrint panel. The script itself is a series of four conditional if statements that assembles the contact name along with proper spacing. Even though the custom field text was initialized in the OnOpen dialog, it needs to be cleared before each name is processed.

Finally, we hid the fields that supply the database data for the program script.

There's more...

Even though we only placed script in the overall report and detail section script dialogs, every section in a report template can have scripts attached. This includes any custom sections you might add. This is good and bad. It provides much flexibility, but it means that you can't treat the scripts as one program. They are in fact several small programs that typically interact. It also can make debugging very difficult.

If you plan on doing much script programming, you will want to make use of the VB Script Language Reference at this URL:

`http://msdn.microsoft.com/en-us/library/d1wf56tt(VS.85).aspx`

Reverse engineering a set of complex scripts

This task is for the serious VB script programmer and you do need a working knowledge of Visual Basic and some programming background.

Rather than trying to build a complex set of scripts, this task will walk through the scripts for the History Summary Classic report. This report has scripts in the history subreport and the main report and values are passed from the subreport to the main report.

Finding the various program scripts in an ACT! report template isn't difficult, all that you need to do is use the edit report scripts option in each location where a script can be placed and you can view all the program scripts. The trick is getting an overview of how the scripts work together to create the finished report. In the History Summary Classic report, counts of specific type of a contacts history types are accumulated for a given date range. What makes the report scripts complex is that the individual contact's count of the tracked history types is done and displayed in the history subreport but the global total of history types is accumulated in the main report.

Getting ready

Because the report template we are working with is one of the standard ACT! Reports, we will start by opening the History Summary Report for editing even though we won't be doing any editing.

How to do it...

1. From any screen in the ACT! program, click on **Reports** in the navigation bar on the left-hand side of the screen.
2. In the list of report templates, right-click on the **History Summary Classic** template and select **Edit Report**.
3. In the field immediately above the **Toolbox**, click the dropdown and select **Histories**.

> Note that the only section expanded in the Histories subreport is the **Footer**. These are the fields that print for each contact in the report.

4. In turn click on each of the fields that show as 0 and take note of the **Name** property. These are custom fields that display the counts accumulated for each contact.

5. Left-click in the blank space below the history subreport sections and then right-click and select **Edit Report Scripts**.
6. Us the dropdown in the **Edit Report Scripts** dialog to select **OnOpen**. The fields we observed in step 4 are being initialized for each contact's histories.

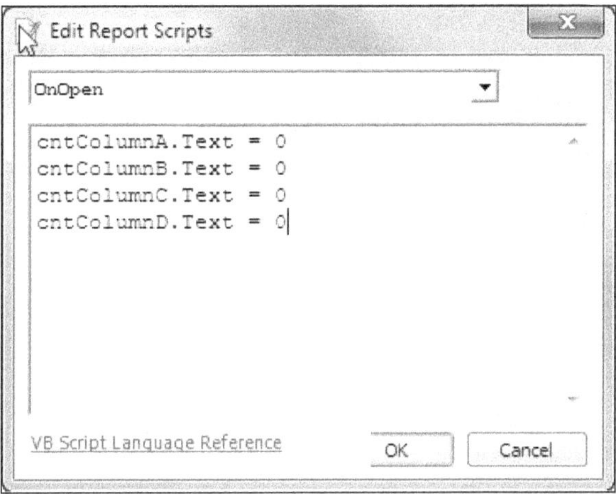

7. Click the **Cancel** button.
8. Left-click on the **Detail** bar and then right-click and select **Edit Report Scripts**.
9. The program script in the **Edit Report Script** dialog are a series of tests of the date in the **Result** field which is a hidden field in the **Detail** section. Anytime a matching history is found, the corresponding count is incremented.

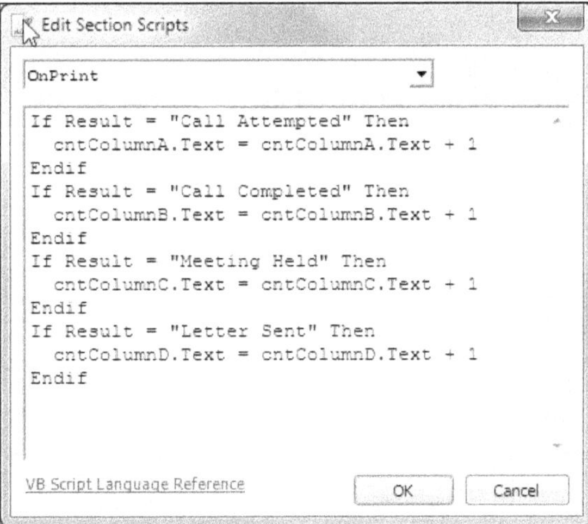

10. Click the **Cancel** button.
11. Left-click in the blank space below the history subreport sections and then right-click and select **Edit Report Scripts**.
12. Us the dropdown in the **Edit Report Scripts** dialog to select **OnClose**. There are two groups of program scripts in the **OnClose** dialog. The order of the groups is important. The first group transfers the counts we accumulated in histories for the contact to custom fields in the main report. After the transfer is made, the count custom fields are cleared.

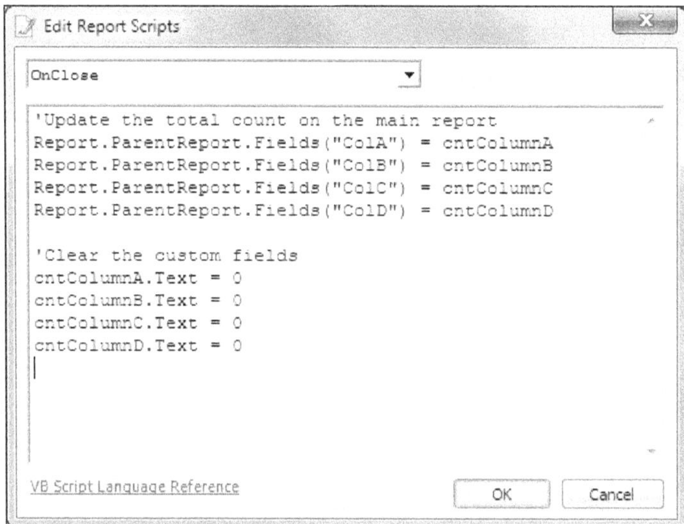

The apostrophe (') is a comment mark and causes everything following it on the carriage return to be ignored by the script interpreter.

13. Click the **Cancel** button.
14. In the field immediately above the **Toolbox**, click the dropdown and select **History Summary Classic (Main)**.

Note that in the main report only, the **Report Footer** and the **Page Header** are expanded. The field labels shown in the **Page Header** align with the fields in the **Histories** subreport footer section.

15. In turn click on each of the fields in the **Report Footer** that show as 0 and take note of the **Name** property. These are custom fields that display the global total for all the contact records processed.
16. At the top of the **Properties** panel, use the dropdown to select the **ColA Custom** field. The **ColA: D** fields are hidden fields in the **Detail** section of the main report. These were the custom fields referenced in the OnClose scripts in the subreport.
17. Left-click on the **Detail** bar and then right-click and select **Edit Report Scripts**.
18. In the **Edit Report Script** dialog, there are two groups of scripts. The top group updated the global totals when the history totals are transferred from the subreport to the main report at the end of processing for each contact record. The second group of scripts resets the custom fields that receive the history totals in preparation for the next contact record.

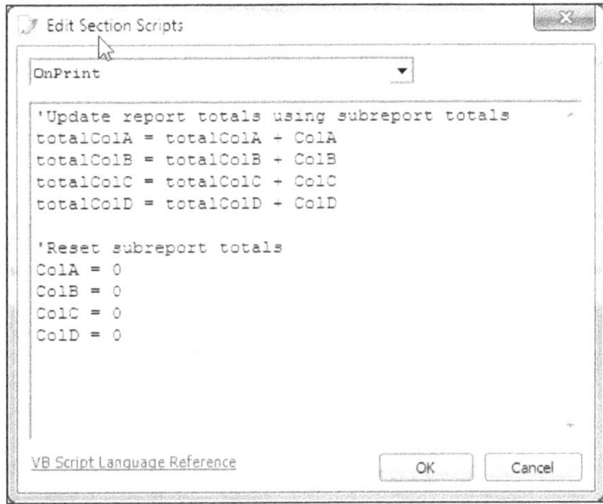

19. Click the **Cancel** button.
20. Close the template without saving.

How it works...

Most of the report templates included with the ACT! program include some program scripts. Before attempting to modify a standard report, you need to know first if it includes program scripts and what do they do so that your modification doesn't interfere with the existing scripts. This task was designed to take you through the process of reverse engineering, a fairly complex set of program scripts. You now should have an understanding of how the History Summary Classic reports work. You should have also picked up some useful tips that you can use when you write your own program scripts.

Several other of the standard reports have complex program scripts and you might want to try reverse engineering a couple of those. One such report is the History: Time Spent report where program scripts are used to convert time in a character field into actual time data type. Another is Won Opportunities by Actual Closing Month where program scripts are used to provide separate totals by the month.

6
Labels and Envelopes

In this chapter, we will cover:

- Editing a standard envelope
- Adding a logo to an envelope
- Creating a custom envelope
- Creating an xx64 label template

Introduction

In this chapter, we will be working with the label and envelope options in the ACT! report editor. The labels and envelopes use a subset of the overall ACT! report editor so most of what was covered in *Chapter 4, Working with the Report Designer* and *Chapter 5, Subreports and Scripting Techniques* regarding fields and field properties also applies to the labels and envelopes. For normal printing, the envelopes and labels are accessed from the File menu and then by choosing Print. Existing envelope and label templates can be opened for editing from the Print dialog, but for creating new templates it's best to go through the Report menu. We will be using that method in these tasks.

After reading this chapter, you will be able to edit or create any envelope or label templates that you would need. While the field functions used with envelopes or labels are the same as with reports, the field spacing requirements are different.

Editing a standard envelope

The number 10 envelope template (or typical local business envelope) supplied with the ACT! program is generally suitable for most users. However there are several common modifications that you may want to make to the standard template. These modifications often include eliminating the return address if you are using envelopes with the return address pre-printed. Another common modification is changing the font type or size.

Getting ready

Because we are starting by editing a standard template, there isn't any preparation required other than to have an ACT! database open.

How to do it...

1. From any screen in the ACT! program, click on the **Report** menu and select **Edit Template**.
2. In the **Open ACT! Report** dialog, click the dropdown where it says ACT! Report Files (`*.rep`) and select ACT! Envelope Files (`*.env`).
3. Double-click on **10.env** (you may not have the extension `.env` showing).
4. Click the **File** menu and select **Save As**. Type `10 Training` for the **File Name**.
5. Click the **Save** button.
6. In the upper-left corner of the template, left-click on the **Custom** field at the top of the return address. Then hold down the *Shift* key and left-click each of the following fields:
    - **My:Company]**
    - **My:Address 1]**
    - **My:Address 2]**
    - **Custom**

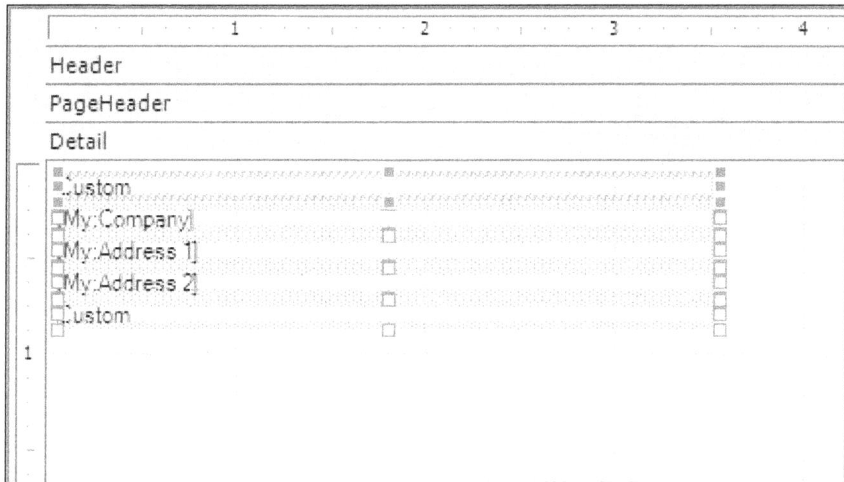

> Do not use any of the click and drag methods for selecting these fields. There are several hidden fields located in this same area and a click and drag to select the fields could also select one or more of the hidden fields.

7. Press the *Delete* key to delete the return address fields from the template.
8. Click on the **Custom** field at the top of the main address.
9. If the **Properties Panel** isn't showing, press the *F4* function key to display the panel.
10. Change the font to **Times New Roman** and the size to **12** point. Verify the **Height** preference is set to `0.19` and **Top** is set to `1.9`.
11. Click on the **C:Company** field.
12. Change to font to **Times New Roman** and the size to **12** point. Verify the **Height** preference is set to `0.19` and **Top** is set to `2.09`. Set **Can Grow** and **Word Wrap** to **No**.
13. Click on the **C:Address 1** field.
14. Change the font to **Times New Roman** and the size to **12** point. Verify the **Height** preference is set to `0.19` and **Top** is set to `2.29`. Set **Can Grow** and **Word Wrap** to **No**.
15. Click on the **C:Address 2** field.
16. Change the font to **Times New Roman** and the size to **12** point. Verify the **Height** preference is set to `0.19` and **Top** is set to `2.49`. Set **Can Grow** and **Word Wrap** to **No**.
17. Click on the **Custom** field at the bottom of the main address.
18. Change the font to **Times New Roman** and the size to **12** point. Verify the **Height** preference is set to `0.19` and **Top** set to `2.69`.

19. Click the **File** menu and select **Save**.
20. Click the **File** menu and select **Exit**.

How it works...

By removing the return address, the envelope template can be used with envelopes with a pre-printed return address. However, because the number 10 envelope template included with the ACT! program doesn't group the hidden fields as we did in *Chapter 4*, but rather scatters them along the top of the template, we need to be careful that we don't include those fields along with the return address fields.

Changing the font size for the main address on the standard number 10 envelope involves little more than selecting the fields and changing the type size. It turns out that while the type size set for the standard template was 10 point, the field size and spacing was more appropriate for 12 point type. We also set the Can Grow and Word Wrap properties for the address field to No as a good practice for addressing envelopes.

Adding a logo to an envelope

For this task we'll assume that the standard number 10 envelope template generally suits your need but that you would like to add you company logo to the return address.

The logo file type that you use for this task, can be any of the standard graphic formats such as BMP, JPG, GIF, and so on. The main task objective is to make room for the logo on the envelope and then insert and size the graphic file. For the purposes of this task, let's use an image file that is available on the system. Logos and images come in a variety of shapes and sizes. We will use a relatively simple rectangle for this task. You will need to modify the measurements that are used to fit your own logo.

Getting ready

As with the previous task, we will start by editing a standard template. There isn't any preparation required other than to have an ACT! database open.

How to do it...

1. From any screen in the ACT! program, click on the **Report** menu and select **Edit Template**.
2. In the **Open ACT! Report** dialog, click the dropdown where it says **ACT! Report Files** (`*.rep`) and select **ACT! Envelope Files** (`*.env`).
3. Double-click on **10.env** (you may not have the extension `.env` showing).

4. Click the **File** menu and select **Save As**. Type `10 Training with Logo` for the **File Name**.
5. Click the **Save** button.
6. In the upper-left corner of the template, left-click on the **Custom** field at the top of the return address. Then hold down the *Shift* key and left-click each of the following fields:
    - **My:Company**
    - **My:Address 1**
    - **My:Address 2**
    - **Custom**
7. Set the **Left** property to **1.5 inches**.
8. In the toolbar, click on the **Picture** tool.
9. Position the crosshair cursor near the upper left corner of the **Detail** section workspace and click and drag down and to the right to create a field that is approximately 1-inch square.
10. In the **Open Image** dialog, navigate to the folder where your logo file is located. Double-click on the logo file.
11. Click on the picture field and set the **Picture Alignment** to **Zoom**.
12. Set the **Left** and **Top properties** to **0.05**.
13. Adjust the **Height** and **Width** properties to size the logo properly for your use. This may involve moving the return address fields left or right as needed.

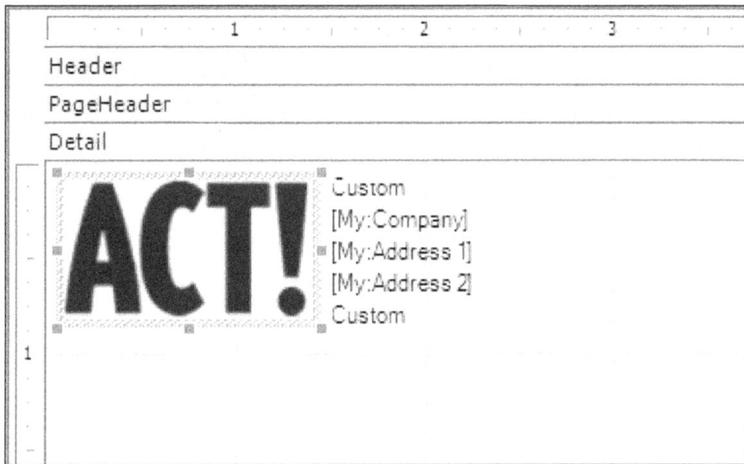

14. Click the **File** menu and select **Save**.
15. Click the **File** menu and select **Exit**.

How it works...

Adding a logo to any envelope is a relatively easy. You first move the existing return address to accommodate the logo image. Because logo sizes vary, you will need to make the move approximate. My suggestion is to leave more space than is needed and move the return address fields back after you sized the logo. Next, add the picture field and add the logo file to the field. The logo will insert to fit the field you defined, which does not typically match the aspect ratio of the logo. This is resolved by setting the picture field picture alignment to zoom, which restores the logo image to its proper aspect ratio. Then set the location, height, and width properties to size the logo the appropriate size and position on the envelope. Finally set the left property on the return address to properly position the actual return address,

Creating a custom envelope

The ACT! program comes with a standard number 10 envelope template and because most printers recognize that envelope size, they print without any problem. Depending on your printer some of the other standard envelope templates provided with the ACT! program may or may not print as desired.

This happens because if the printer doesn't recognize the envelope size, the page setup for the envelope defaults to 8.5 X 11 letter size with zero margins and the envelope prints in the upper left corner of the page. This typically doesn't match where your printer would feed the envelopes. To further confuse things, you can start a custom envelope of any size but if the printer doesn't recognize that size, the page setup will default to letter.

It turns out the best way to create a custom envelope is to start with the 8.5 X 11 letter size and adjust the margins to create a printing area on the sheet that corresponds to where envelopes feed with your printer. For the purposes of this task, let's use a greeting card envelope that is five-inches tall by 7.5 inches wide. We will also use the envelope feed positioning of face down on the right-hand side of the feed tray with the envelope flap toward the center of the feed tray.

Getting ready

Because we will be creating a new template, there isn't any preparation required other than have an ACT! database open.

How to do it...

1. From any screen in the ACT! program, click on **Reports** in the navigation bar on the left-hand side of the screen.
2. Under **Related Tasks** in the navigation bar click on **New Report Template**.
3. In the **New Report** dialog, click on **Contact Envelopes** and then click the **OK** button.

4. In the **New Envelope** dialog, select **Custom** in the **Select an envelope size** field and set the **Height** to `11.00` and **Width** to `8.50` and click the **OK** button.

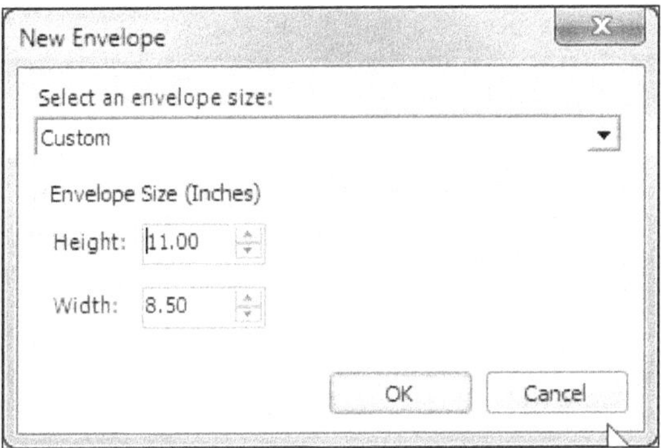

5. Click the **File** menu and select Save As. Type `Custom Envelope Training` for the **File Name**.
6. Click the **Save** button.
7. In the **Properties Panel**, use the dropdown to select **Custom Envelope Training Report** and set the **Font** to **Times New Roman**, and size to **12** point.
8. Click on the **File** menu and select **Page Setup**.
9. In the **Page Setup** dialog, set the margins to **Left** `0.25`, **Right** `3.5`, **Top** `3.5` and **Bottom** `0.25`. Click the **OK** button.

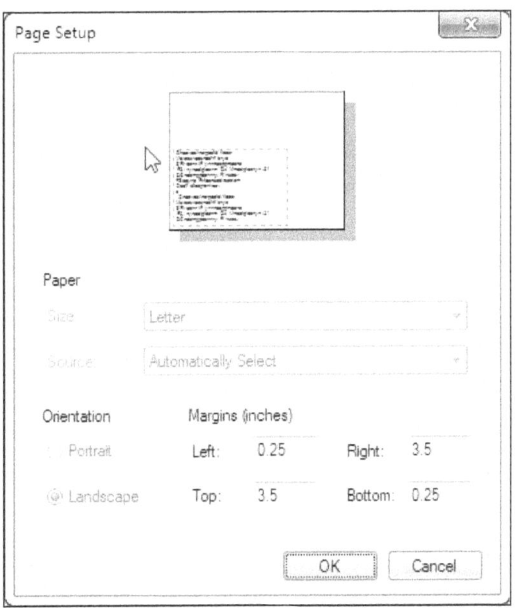

Setting the margins requires that on the Left and Bottom you allow for the non-printing area on your printer. The Top and Right margins position the workspace we will use to the lower left portion of the letter sheet. This corresponds to the envelope we are using.

10. Click on the **Detail** bar and set the **Height** property to `4.75`.
11. In the toolbar, click on the **Field** tool. Close to the upper-left corner of the detail section, use the crosshair cursor to click and drag to create a field about one-inch long.
12. In the **Select Field** dialog, change the **Select a record type** to `My Record` and uncheck **Include a label**.

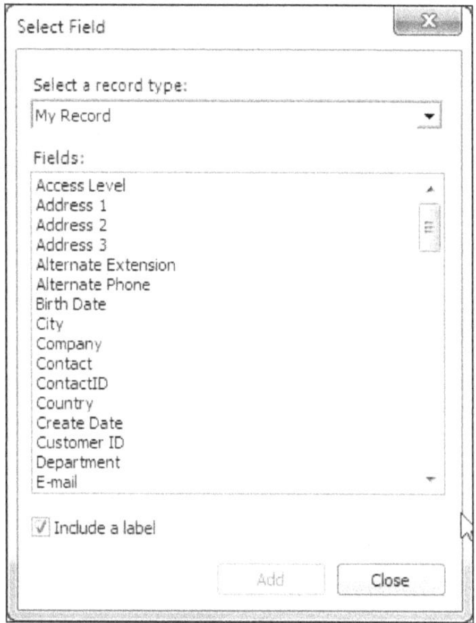

13. Double click on the following fields:
    - **Company**
    - **Address 1**
    - **Address 2**
    - **City**
    - **State**
    - **ZIP Code**
14. Click the **Close** button.

15. Place the cursor in the left margin of the workspace, above the **My:Company** field so that it turns into an arrow and drag down to select all the fields to be used for the return address.
16. Set the type size to **8 point bold**. Set the properties for all these fields to **Can Grow**: **No**, **Can Shrink**: **Yes**, **Word Wrap**: **No**, **Alignment**: **Left Middle**, **Height**: `0.14`, **Left:** `0.05`, and **Width**: `2.0`.
17. Click on the **Detail** bar and then on the **My:Company** field and set the **Top** property to `0.1`.
18. Click on the **My:Address 1** field and set the **Top property** to `0.25`.
19. Click on the **My:Address 2** field and set the **Top property** to `0.4`.
20. In the toolbar, click on the **System Field** tool. Below the fields in the detail section, use the crosshair cursor to click and drag to create a field about one-inch long.
21. In the **Select System Field** dialog, uncheck **Include a label** and double-click on **Custom**.
22. Click the **Close** button.
23. Click on the **Custom** field and set the type size to `8` point bold. Set the properties for the field to **Alignment**: **Left Middle**, **Height**: `0.14`, **Left**: `0.05`, **Width**: `2.0`, and **Top**: `0.55`.
24. Click on the **My:City** field and set the properties to **Visible**: **False**, **Height**: `0.01`, **Left**: `6.75`, **Top**: `0.01`, and **Width**: `0.2`.
25. Click on the **My:statefield** and set the properties to **Visible**: **False**, **Height**: `0.01`, **Left**: `6.75`, **Top**: `0.03`, and **Width**: `0.2`.
26. Click on the **My:ZIP Code** field and set the properties to **Visible**: **False**, **Height**: `0.01`, **Left**: `6.75`, **Top**: `0.05`, and **Width**: `0.2`.
27. Click on the **Detail** bar and then right-click and select **Edit Report Scripts**.
28. Type the following line of script code:

```
Custom1.text = City1&", "&State1&" "&ZIPCode1
```

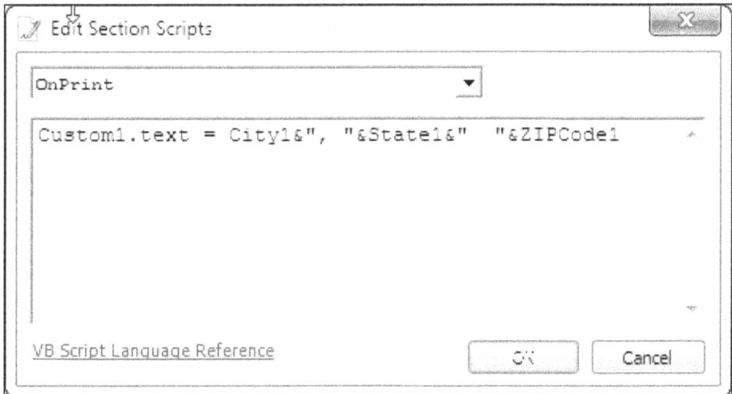

This is the script line for the return address. Because envelopes have a limited number of fields on them, I didn't rename the field objects. Note that each of the field names has `1` as the last character. This is automatically added by the report editor.

29. Click the **OK** button.
30. Click the **File** menu and select **Save** to save your work before going on.
31. In the toolbar, click on the **Field** tool. About 2.5-inches from the top and left side of the detail section, use the crosshair cursor to click and drag to create a field about two-inches long.
32. In the **Select Field** dialog, make sure the **Select a record type** is set to `Contact` and uncheck **Include a label**.

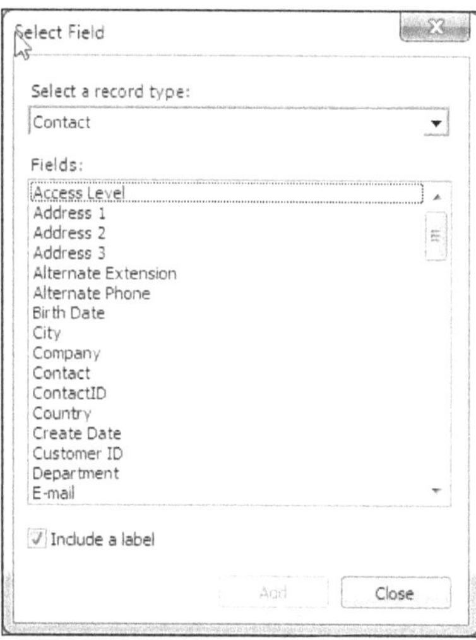

33. Double-click on the following fields:
    - **Contact**
    - **Company**
    - **Address 1**
    - **Address 2**
    - **Address 3**
    - **City**
    - **State**
    - **ZIP Code**
34. Click the **Close** button.

35. Place the cursor in the left margin of the workspace, above the **C:Contact** field so that it turns into an arrow and drag down to select all the field to be used for the main address.
36. Set the properties for all these fields to **Can Grow**: **No**, **Can Shrink**: **Yes**, **Word Wrap**: **No**, **Alignment**: **Left Middle**, **Height**: `0.19`, **Left**: `3.0`, and **Width**: `3.0`.
37. Click on the **Detail** bar and then on the **C:Contact** field and set the **Top** property to `2.0`.
38. Click on the **C:Company** field and set the **Top** property to `2.2`.
39. Click on the **C:Address 1** field and set the **Top** property to `2.4`.
40. Click on the **C:Address 2** field and set the **Top** property to `2.6`.
41. Click on the **C:Address 3** field and set the **Top** property to 2.8.
42. In the toolbar click on the **System Field** tool. Below the main address fields in the detail section, use the crosshair cursor to click and drag to create a field about two-inches long.
43. In the **Select System Field** dialog, uncheck **Include a label**, and double-click on **Custom**.
44. Click on the **Close** button.
45. Click on the **Custom** field and set the properties for the field to **Alignment**: **Left Middle**, **Height**: `0.19`, **Left**: `2.0`, **Width**: `3.0`, and **Top**: `3.0`.
46. Click on the **C:City** field and set the properties to **Visible**: **False**, **Height**: `0.01`, **Left**: `6.75`, **Top**: `0.07`, and **Width**: `0.2`.
47. Click on the **C:statefield** and set the properties to **Visible**: **False**, **Height**: `0.01`, **Left**: `6.75`, **Top**: `0.09`, and **Width**: `0.2`.
48. Click on the **C:ZIP** Code field and set the properties to **Visible**: **False**, **Height**: `0.01`, **Left**: `6.75`, **Top**: `0.11`, and **Width**: `0.2`.
49. Click on the **Detail** bar and then right-click and select **Edit Report Scripts**.
50. Type the following line of script code:

```
Custom2.text = City2&", "&State2&" "&ZIPCode2
```

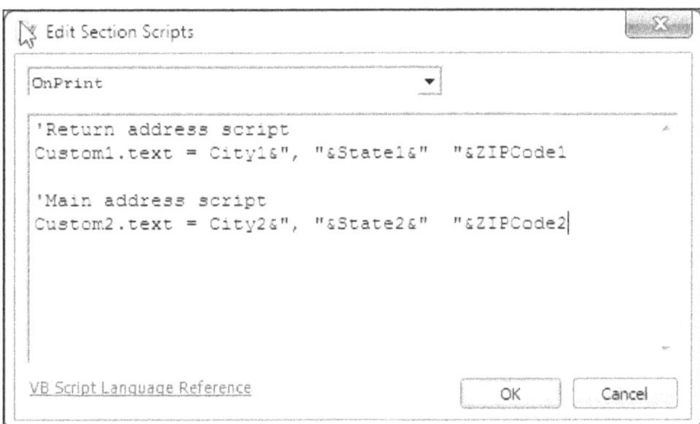

This is the script for both the return and main address. Note that two comment lines have been added to help identify the scripts. The comments are optional but they are helpful if you need to edit the script in the future.

51. Click the **File** menu and select **Save** to save your the completed envelope template.

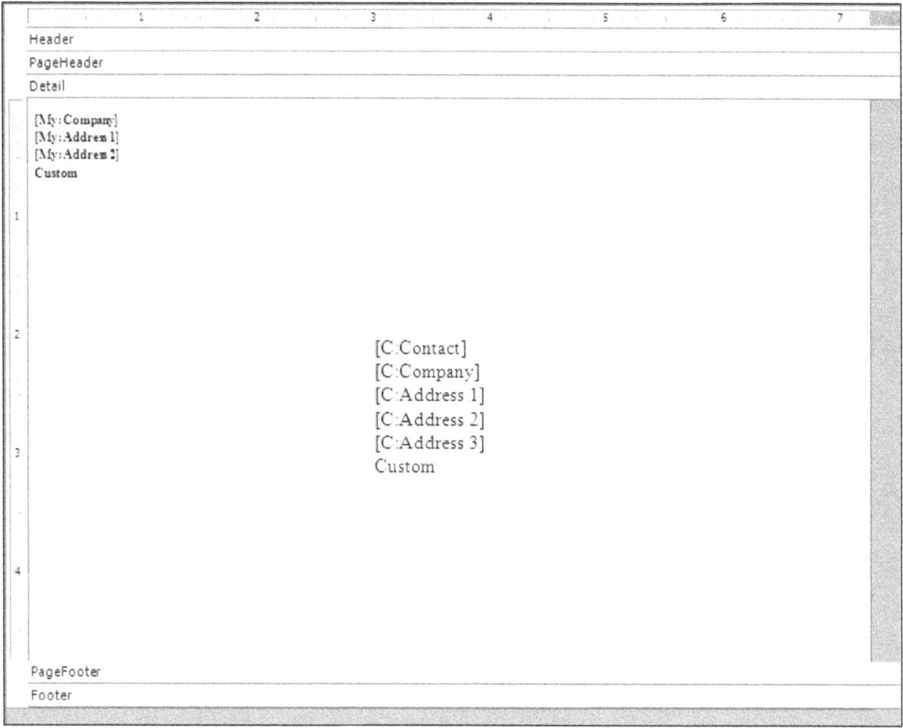

How it works...

Most of the operations covered in this task are repeats of operations covered in *Chapters 4* and *5*. The main thing new thing was the initial creation of the workspace for the custom envelope. The hardest part of creating the workspace is translating the way your printer feeds and prints envelopes into the proper space on the letter sheet. Most printers feed letter paper in the portrait position even though envelopes generally print in landscape relative to the letter sheet. This means that your envelope workspace on the template needs to be flushed with the left-hand side of the letter sheet when you do the page setup.

Here's a tip on creating the workspace: make a rectangle in the report editor the size of your envelope and do a print preview to see where it appears on the letter sheet. Using the basic information in this task you can easily create any size custom envelope template needed.

Creating an xx64 label template

Editing any of the standard labels for font changes or inserting a logo is much the same as what was done with the envelopes and won't be repeated here. However, the ACT! program doesn't include a template for the commonly used Avery shipping label xx64. (Avery uses the first two numbers to designate the label material and the last two numbers to designate the size.) Your printer may or may not have the dimensions built in for the xx64 label. The dimensioning provided for some of the labels and often isn't the best to have the type align to the label. For that reason, we will be skipping any specific label selection and using the preferences in the report editor to define the label.

Getting ready

Because we will be creating a new template, there isn't any preparation required other than to have an ACT! database open.

How to do it...

1. From any screen in the ACT! program, click on **Reports** in the navigation bar on the left side of the screen.
2. Under **Related Tasks** in the navigation bar click on **New Report Template**.
3. In the **New Report** dialog, click on **Contact Labels** and then click the **OK** button.
4. Click the **OK** button in the **Create Label** dialog.
5. Click the **File** menu and select **Save As**. Type `Custom xx64 Label Training` for the **File Name**.
6. Click the **Save** button.
7. In the **Properties Panel**, use the dropdown to select **Custom xx64 Label Training Report** and set the **Font** to **Times New Roman 12pt**.

8. Set the **Label** and **Layout** properties as follows:
   - **Columns**: `2`
   - **Horizontal Space**: `0.16`
   - **Vertical Space**: `0`
   - **Width**: `4`
   - **Margin Bottom**: `0`
   - **Margin Left**: `0.17`
   - **Margin Right**: `0.17`
   - **Orientation**: **Portrait**
   - **Top Margin**: `0.5`

Properties

Custom xx64 Label Training Report

Appearance	
Font	Times New Roman, 12pt
Picture	(none)
Picture Alignment	Center Middle
Show Picture	AllPages
Behavior	
Maximum Pages	0
Label	
Columns	3
HorizontalSpace	0.16
VerticalSpace	0
Width	4
Layout	
Margin Bottom	0
Margin Left	0.17
Margin Right	0.17
Orientation	Portrait
Top Margin	0.5

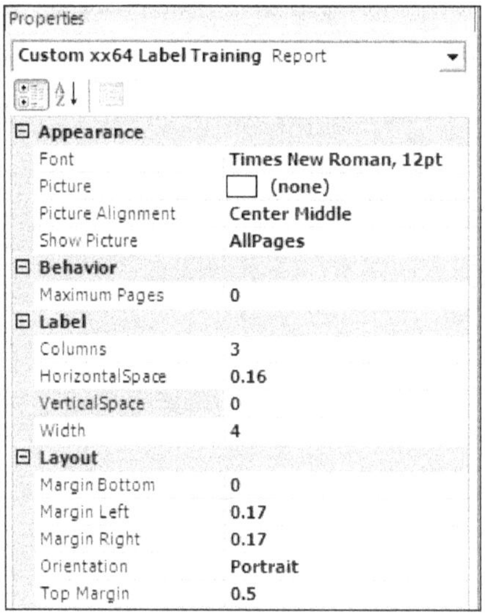

9. Click on the **Detail** bar and set the **Height** property to `3.33`.
10. Click on the **File** menu and select **Save** to save the layout.
11. In the toolbar click on the **Field** tool. Close to the upper left corner of the detail section, use the crosshair cursor to click and drag to create a field about one-inch long.
12. In the **Select Field** dialog, change the **Select a record type** to `My Record` and uncheck **Include a label**.

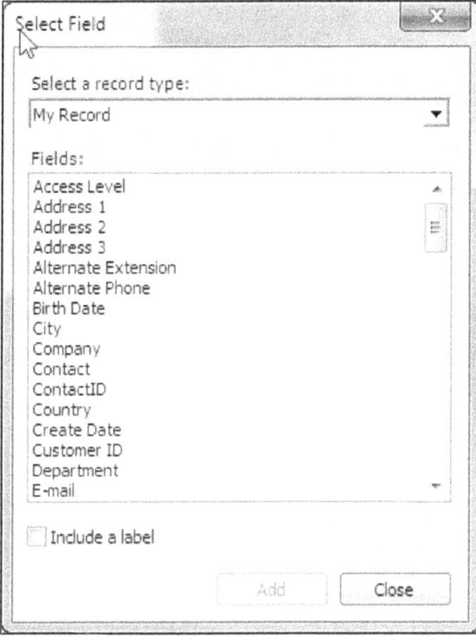

13. Double-click on the following fields:
    - **Company**
    - **Address 1**
    - **Address 2**
    - **City**
    - **State**
    - **ZIP Code**
14. Click the **Close** button.
15. Place the cursor in the left margin of the workspace above the **My:Company** field so that it turns into an arrow and drag down to select all the field to be used for the return address.
16. Set the type size to `10` point. Set the properties for all these fields to **Can Grow**: **No**, **Can Shrink**: **Yes**, **Word Wrap**: **No**, **Alignment**: **Center Middle**, **Height**: `0.16`, **Left**: `0.75`, and **Width**: `2.5`.
17. Click on the **Detail** bar and then on the **My:Company** field and set the **Top** property to `0.1`.
18. Click on the **My:Address 1** field and set the **Top** property to `0.27`.
19. Click on the **My:Address 2** field and set the **Top** property to `0.44`.
20. In the toolbar click on the **System Field** tool. Below the fields in the **Detail** section, use the crosshair cursor to click and drag to create a field about one-inch long.

21. In the **Select System Field** dialog, uncheck **Include a label** and double-click on **Custom**.
22. Click the **Close** button.
23. Click on the **Custom** field and set the type size to `10` point. Set the properties for the field to **Alignment**: **Center Middle**, **Height**: `0.16`, **Left**: `0.75`, **Width**: `2.5`, and **Top**: `0.61`.
24. Click on the **My:City** field and set the properties to **Visible**: **False**, **Height**: `0.01`, **Left**: `3.5`, **Top**: `0.01`, and **Width**: `0.2`.
25. Click on the **My:statefield** and set the properties to **Visible**: **False**, **Height**: `0.01`, **Left**: `3.5`, **Top**: `0.03`, and **Width**: `0.2`.
26. Click on the **My:ZIP Code** field and set the properties to **Visible**: **False**, **Height**: `0.01`, **Left**: `3.5`, **Top**: `0.05`, and **Width**: `0.2`.
27. In the toolbar, click on the **Text** tool. Close to the upper-left corner of the detail section, use the crosshair cursor to click and drag to create a field about 0.5-inch squared.
28. Set the **Font** to **Tahoma**, **Bold**, **18pt**. In the **Text** property type **From:**.
29. Set the properties to **Alignment**: **Left Middle**, **Height**: `0.3`, **Left**: `0.1`, **Top**: `0.1`, and **Width**: `0.75`.
30. Click on the **Detail** bar and then right-click and select **Edit Report Scripts**.
31. Type the following line of script code:

```
Custom1.text = City1&", "&State1&" "&ZIPCode1
```

32. Click the **OK** button.
33. In the toolbar, click on the **Rectangle** tool. Below the return address fields, use the crosshair cursor to click and drag to create a rectangle about one-inch long.
34. Click on the rectangle and set the properties to **Background Color**: **Black**, **Left**: `0`, **Height**: `0.05`, **Top**: `0.9`, and **Width**: `4.0`.
35. Click the **File** menu and select **Save** to save your work before going on.
36. In the toolbar, click on the **Field** tool. About 0.5 inches under the divider bar in the detail section, use the crosshair cursor to click and drag to create a field about two-inches long.
37. In the **Select Field** dialog, make sure the **Select a record type** is set to `Contact` and uncheck **Include a label**.
38. Double-click on the following fields:
    - **Contact**
    - **Company**
    - **Address 1**
    - **Address 2**

- **Address 3**
- **City**
- **State**
- **ZIP Code**

39. Click the **Close** button.
40. Place the cursor in the left margin of the workspace above the **C:Contact** field so that it turns into an arrow and drag down to select all the field to be used for the main address.
41. Set the **Font** to **Times New Roman**, **12** point.
42. Set the properties for all these fields to **Can Grow**: **No**, **Can Shrink**: **Yes**, **Word Wrap**: **No**, **Alignment**: **Left Middle**, **Height**: `0.19`, **Left**: `0.5`, and **Width**: `3.0`.
43. Click on the **Detail** bar and then on the **C:Contact** field and set the **Top** property to `1.5`.
44. Click on the **C:Company** field and set the **Top** property to `1.7`.
45. Click on the **C:Address 1** field and set the **Top** property to `1.9`.
46. Click on the **C:Address 2** field and set the **Top** property to `2.1`.
47. Click on the **C:Address 3** field and set the **Top** property to `2.3`.
48. Click on the **C:City** field and set the properties to **Visible**: **False**, **Height**: `0.01`, **Left**: `3.5`, **Top**: `0.07`, and **Width**: `0.2`.
49. Click on the **C:statefield** and set the properties to **Visible**: **False**, **Height**: `0.01`, **Left**: `3.5`, **Top**: `0.09`, and **Width**: `0.2`.
50. Click on the **C:ZIP Code** field and set the properties to **Visible**: **False**, **Height**: `0.01`, **Left**: `3.5`, **Top**: `0.11`, and **Width**: `0.2`.
51. In the toolbar, click on the **System Field** tool. Below the main address fields in the detail section, use the crosshair cursor to click and drag to create a field about two-inches long.
52. In the **Select System Field** dialog, uncheck **Include a label** and double-click on **Custom**.
53. Click the **Close** button.
54. Click on the **Custom** field and set the **Font** to **Times New Roman 12** point and the properties for the field to **Alignment**: **Left Middle**, **Height**: `0.19`, **Left**: `0.5`, **Width**: `3.0`, and **Top**: `2.5`.
55. Click on the **Detail** bar and then right-click and select **Edit Report Scripts**.

56. Type the following line of script code:

```
Custom2.text = City2&", "&State2&" "&ZIPCode2
```

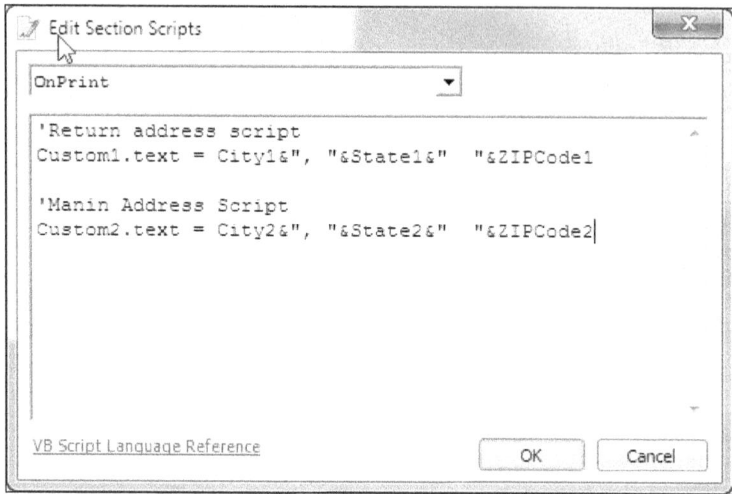

57. Click on the **OK** button.
58. Right-click on the **From** text field and select **Copy**. Right-click again and click **Paste**.
59. Drag the copy down below the divider bar.
60. Click on the copy and change the **Text** to **To**: and se the properties to **Top**: `1.0`, **Left**: `0.1`, and **Width**: `0.5`.
61. Click the **File** menu and select **Save** to save your the completed envelope template.

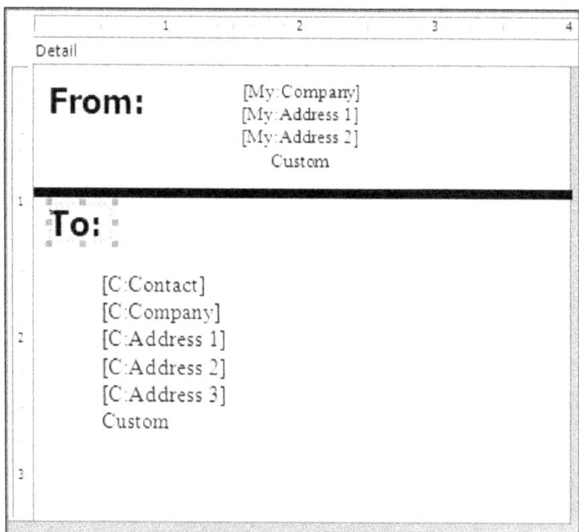

How it works...

As with the custom envelope, most of the operations in this task were repeats of ones used in previous tasks. Creating the basic label format was the main thing new here. The reason for choosing to show how to define the format in the report editor is that it was more accurate and it will accommodate any style sheet, including things such as name tag sheets in addition to labels. The best way to get the values for the format is to measure an actual sheet.

7

Working with the ACT! Dashboards

In this chapter, we will cover:

- Getting familiar with the Dashboard layouts
- Exploring Dashboard components
- Accessing Dashboard Data
- Copying a Dashboard to the clipboard
- Printing a hard copy of the Dashboard
- Setting Dashboards as the default startup preference

Introduction

One of the coolest new features of ACT! is the addition of the **Dashboard**. A Dashboard allows you to access key information in the form of a graphical interface. You can filter a Dashboard so that it contains just the information you need, or you can tweak the various elements of a Dashboard to give it a different look. Administrators and Managers of your ACT! database can create brand new Dashboards if they're required.

If you want more details about the information you see in a Dashboard, you can drill-down into the Dashboard with a simple double-click to access all the juicy details. At that point, you can edit or add to your information and the Dashboard will update automatically.

You can even print out a hard copy of a Dashboard to preserve the contents for posterity. Because many of the Dashboards consist of pie charts and graphs, you might even want to copy one of them and paste it into other applications such as Word, Excel, or PowerPoint.

Getting familiar with the Dashboard layouts

Quite simply, a Dashboard is a graphical interface that gives you a visual snapshot of a part of your business. ACT! Dashboards let you view and work with the various information contained in your database in one easy-to-access location. Dashboards can take the form of charts, graphs, or even lists. Dashboards are associated with a database and not a user; therefore all users share the same Dashboards. However, you can select your own Dashboard view in much the same way that you can select a layout. You can also filter the information that is shown in your Dashboard.

A Dashboard consists of two parts:

- **The Dashboard layout**: The Dashboard layout determines which Dashboard components you see and how the filters are set. ACT! comes with six Dashboard layouts. However, Managers and Administrators can create additional Dashboard layouts using the Dashboard Designer or make permanent changes to the existing ones.
- **Dashboard components**: Each Dashboard layout consists of one or more **components**. A component displays different types of data from the ACT! database. For example, a Dashboard layout might include a component that lists a user's top 10 current sales opportunities, another component that graphs the activities of a specific user, and a component that displays a pie chart of the company's current pipeline. A layout can have a maximum of six components.

Getting ready

In order to really take advantage of the ACT! Dashboard, you'll need to make sure that your database contains a variety of information. Specifically you'll need to make sure that your database contains a few Contacts, Activities, and Opportunities if you're going to view any of those Dashboards.

How to do it...

1. Click the **Dashboard** icon on ACT!'s navigation bar. The following screenshot shows you an example of the default Dashboard page:

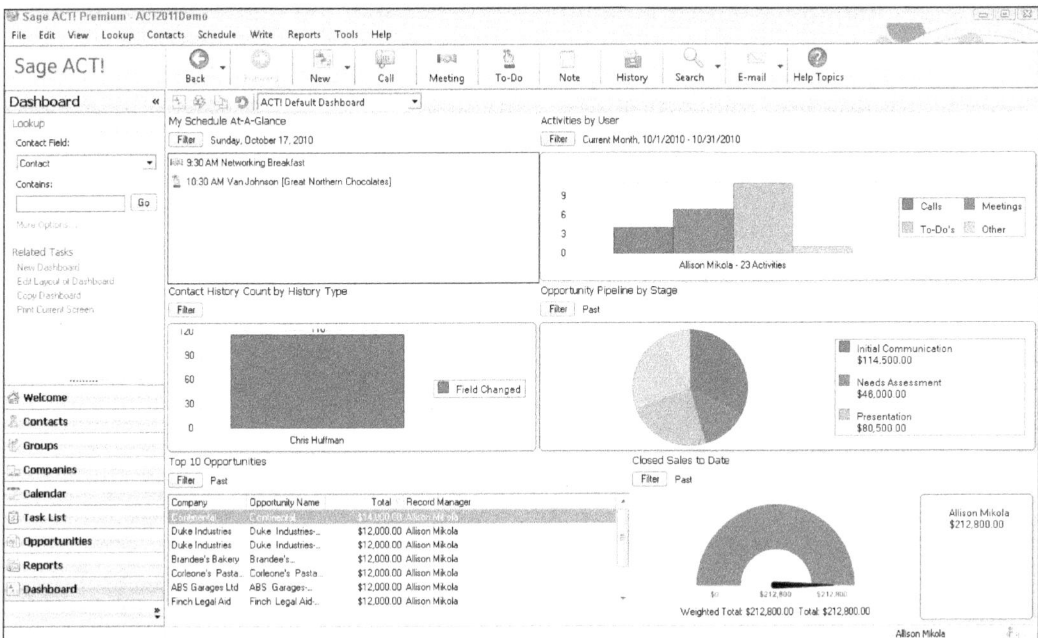

2. Choose the Dashboard layout you want from the Dashboard drop-down list, at the top-left side of the Dashboard.

How it works...

Many of the layouts consist of the exact same components. However, the components in each of the layouts are filtered differently, giving the layouts a bit of variety.

There's more...

Out of the box there are five Dashboard layouts:

- **ACT! Activities Dashboard**: Shows the activities of the user currently signed into ACT!, like the one you see in the following screenshot:

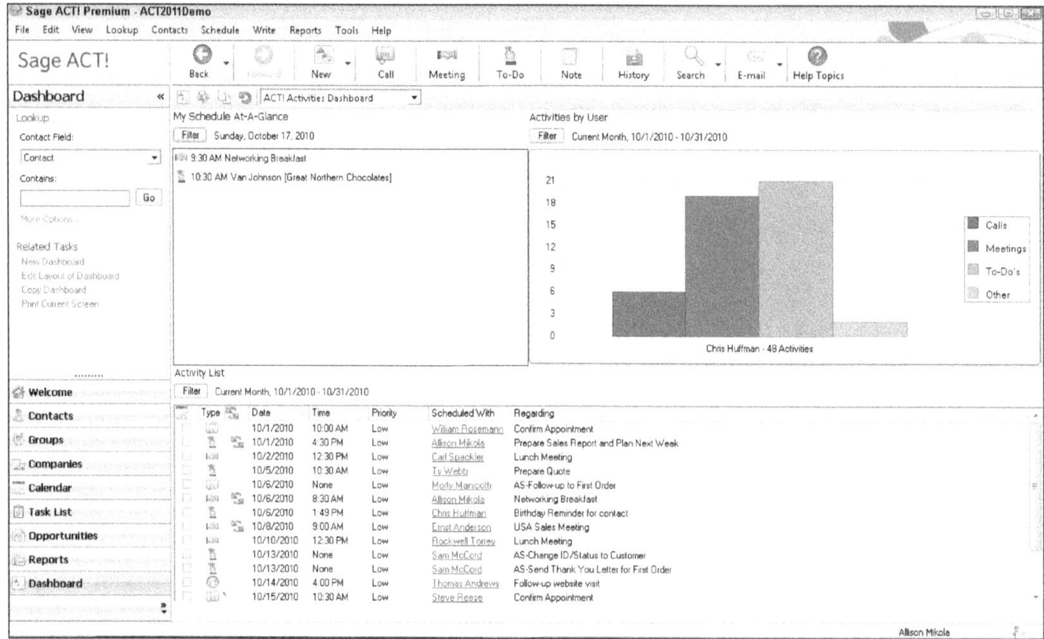

- **ACT! Administration Dashboard**: Lists the database users and shows when they've logged in and out of the database. Also lists any remote sync users, the date of their list sync, and how many days they have before their remote database *expires* if they don't synchronize.
- **ACT! Contact Dashboard**: Gives you a list of recently created contacts, recently edited contacts, and the number of fields that have changed.
- **ACT! Default Dashboard**: Includes three activity and three opportunity components.
- **ACT! Opportunities Dashboard**: Provides you with four different opportunity components including sales analysis by stage, value, and product.

Each Dashboard layout is actually a file ending with the `.dsh` extension. You'll find them safely filed in the Dashboards sub-folder of the database files folder associated with your database.

Accessing information from Dashboards

Once you've become familiar with the various Dashboard layouts your next step is to start exploring the components found in each layout to see what data they contain. The components are generally arranged in a grid of two columns of three rows for a total of six components per Dashboard layout.

The basic components include:

- **My Schedule At-A-Glance**: Found on the Default and Activities Dashboards, this component lists your activities of the current user for the current day.
- **Activities by User**: Found on the Default and Activities Dashboards, this component displays the activities for the current user for the current month, sorted by type, in a bar chart. The total numbers of activities are shown in the following screenshot. In addition you can hover your mouse over a bar section to see the number of activities for that activity type.

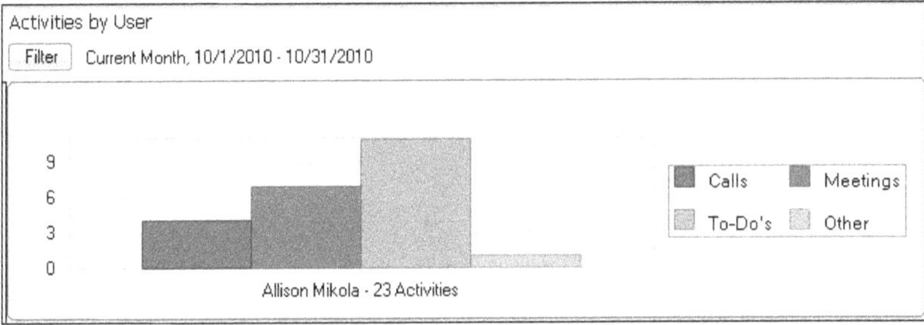

- **Activity List**: Found on the Activities Dashboard, this component is identical to the My Schedule At-A-Glance components, except that it lists all the activities for the current month.
- **Opportunity Pipeline by Stage**: Found on the Opportunities and Default Dashboards, this component displays your open opportunities in the ACT! Sales Cycle process for the current month sorted by stage, in a pie chart and includes a recap on the side like the one you see in the following screenshot:

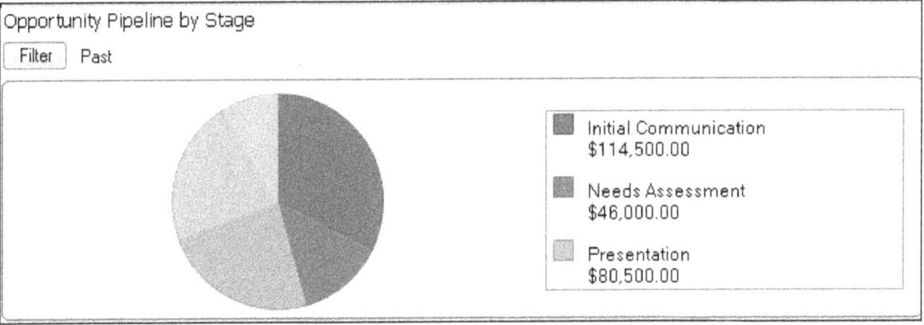

- **Contact History Count by User Type**: Found on the Contacts Dashboard this component displays history items created by database users within a specified number of days similar to what's shown in the following screenshot:

- **Opportunities - Open by Product**: Found on the Opportunities Dashboard, the component displays a pie chart of the open opportunities by product and by user.
- **Top 10 Opportunities**: Found on the Opportunities and Default Dashboards, this component displays a list, by company and opportunity name, of the top ten open opportunities in the ACT! Sales Cycle process for the current month.
- **Closed Sales to Date**: Found on the Opportunities and Default Dashboards, this component displays the weighted and total value of opportunities in the ACT! Sales Cycle process, you closed and *won* in the form of a chart. Optionally you can customize the component to indicate a sales goal like the one shown in the following screenshot:

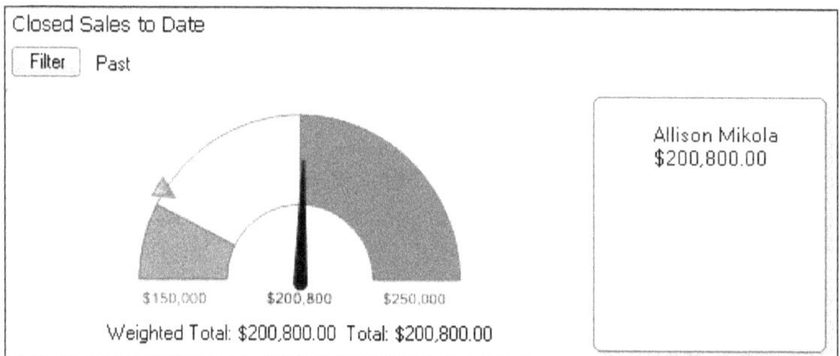

Getting ready

You can access the information that you see in Dashboard components in order to change it or see additional details. You just need to make sure that your database is populated with data that corresponds with the component that you're working with.

How to do it...

1. Click the **Dashboard** icon on ACT!'s navigation bar. Choose the Dashboard layout you want from the Dashboard drop-down list at the top left-hand side of the Dashboard.
2. Choose one of the following options:
   - Click a component to access the supporting data in a chart or graph.
   - Double-click to access the information about a list item.
   - Right-click on a List component and choose **Create Lookup** to create a lookup of the contacts referenced in the component.
3. Click the **Back** icon on the icon bar to return to the Dashboard view.

How it works...

Each component works a little differently. And some components don't do anything, no matter how or how often you click them. For example, the **Contact History Count by History Type**, **Recently Edited Contacts**, and the **Opportunities – Open by Product** components just sit there like a bump on the log.

Here's a list to let you know what you can expect from the various components:

- **My Schedule At-A-Glance or Activity List**: Double-click an activity to open the **Schedule Activity** dialog box
- **Activities by User**: Click a single bar to display the **Task List** that is filtered to show the same data as the component
- **Opportunity Pipeline by Stage, Closed Sales to Date**: Click the chart to display the **Opportunities List** that is filtered to show the same data as the component
- **Top 10 Opportunities**: Double-click to open the **Detail** view of the selected opportunity
- **Closed Sales to Date Gauge**: Click anywhere to display an **Opportunity List** that is filtered to show the same data as the component

There's more...

Not sure whether or not to click or double-click? You'll notice that your cursor changes into the form of a hand when you hover it over a chart or graph. That's your sign that you need only to render a single-click in order to zoom in on that component.

Customizing Dashboard columns

The various list view components may not look as jazzy as their more graphical counterparts but they do give you one additional useful piece of functionality, namely the ability to change the columns that are displayed. Simply right-click in the list and choose **Customize Columns...**. The corresponding dialog window appears like the one in the following screenshot. Select the columns that you want the component to display from the **Available fields:** list, and then click the single right-pointing arrow to move the field to the **Show as columns in this order:** list.

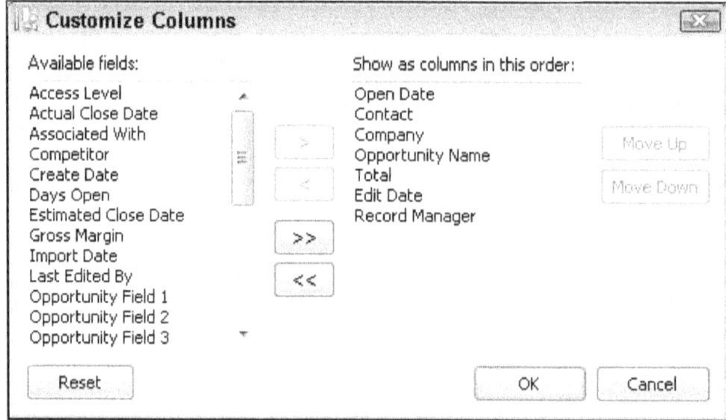

If a component appears to be blank it's because none of the data in your database matches the filtering criteria of that component. As you add additional information to your database that is pertinent to that component, you'll see that the information will appear magically.

Refreshing the Dashboards

From time-to-time, you may find that your Dashboard looks exactly the same as it did before you drilled down into it to change the underlying data. Sometimes the Dashboards don't **refresh** automatically to show the changed data; in those cases you'll have to refresh the data yourself. You can do so by simply clicking the **Refresh** icon that you see on the Dashboard's icon bar.

Copying Dashboard information to other products

If a picture is worth a thousand words then a well-designed Dashboard might be worth a million. If you like what you see in one of the Dashboards or even in a single component, you might want to share it with others by pasting it into a PowerPoint presentation or Word document to add a little pizzazz to your next presentation.

Getting ready

You'll want to make sure that you have already added the necessary information to ACT!. For example, if your goal is to show off your company pipeline, you'll need to make sure that you have the supporting opportunity records in ACT!.

How to do it...

1. Click the Dashboard icon on ACT!'s navigation bar.
2. Choose the Dashboard layout you want from the Dashboard drop-down list at the top-left side of the Dashboard.
3. Choose one of the following options:
    - **To copy the entire Dashboard into the Windows clipboard**: Click the **Copy** icon on the Dashboard menu bar
    - **To copy a single component into the Windows clipboard**: Right-click on the component and choose **Copy To Clipboard** from the contextual menu
4. Open the target program, and choose **Paste** from the **Edit** menu.

How it works...

When you copy a Dashboard or one of its components, it goes automatically to the Windows clipboard where it will remain until you replace it with another item.

There's more...

Once you copy an item into the Windows clipboard, you can continue to paste it into as many places as you'd like.

Printing Dashboards

Dashboards are **dynamic** which means that they change as your data changes. For example, the Dashboard you see on Monday may not look at all like the Dashboard you viewed on Friday. Although you can save a Dashboard layout, you can't save the current information found in that Dashboard. Consequently, the only way you can truly save the contents of a Dashboard for future generations is by making a hard copy of it.

Getting ready

Because a Dashboard is simply a reflection of your current data, you'll want to make sure that you have entered all pertinent data into your ACT! database.

How to do it...

1. Click the Dashboard icon on ACT!'s navigation bar.
2. Choose the Dashboard layout you want from the Dashboard drop-down list at the top-left side of the Dashboard.
3. Choose one of the following options:
   - **To print the entire Dashboard**: Click the **File** menu, choose **Quick Print Current Window**, select the **Print orientation** and **Print sizing** options like the ones you see in the following screenshot and then click **OK**:

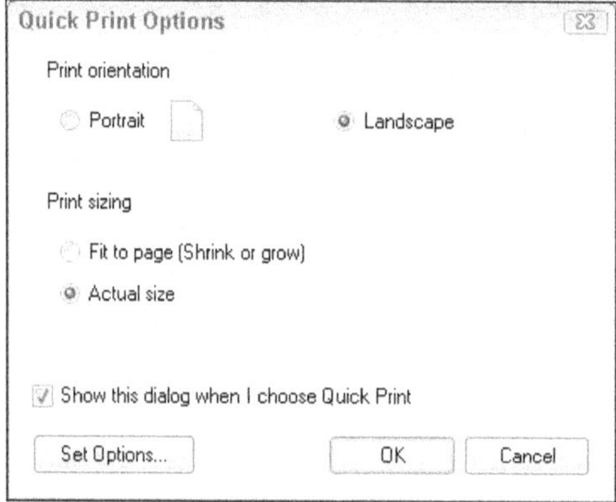

   - **To print a single component**: Right-click on the component and select **Print** from the contextual menu.

How it works...

Once you send the Dashboard or the Dashboard component to the printer you'll be able to apply any of the printer options just as you would with any other document.

There's more...

Unfortunately, although you can print all of the Dashboards, you can't print all of the individual components. Moreover, there doesn't seem to be a whole lot of logic as to which components will print. For example, some of the list components print and others don't. The only advice we can offer is to try each one out for yourself!

Making Dashboards the default startup preference

If you really start to feel that Dashboards are the greatest thing since sliced bread, you can change the default startup preference so that the Dashboards are the first thing you see when you open up your ACT! database.

Getting ready

You can only change your startup preferences if you've fired up ACT! and have a database open.

How to do it...

1. Click **Preferences** from the **Tools** menu.
2. Click the **Startup** tab.
3. Click the **Startup view** drop-down in the **Log On settings** section and choose Dashboard. Your screen should look pretty much like the following screenshot:

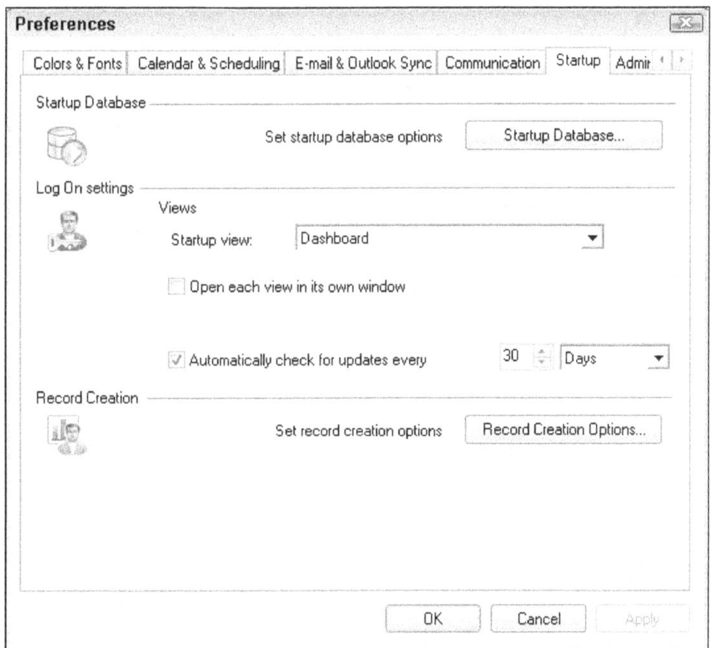

4. Click **OK** to save your changes.

How it works...

The next time you open ACT! it will automatically open to the Dashboard view.

There's more...

Smart reader that you are, you might have noticed that although you indicated Dashboard as the Startup **view** preference, you weren't asked to indicate your **layout** preference. Indicating the Startup Dashboard layout is a bit trickier—or perhaps *stickier*.

Once you have changed your Startup preference to Dashboard, you can experiment a bit by choosing a Dashboard layout and then closing your database. You'll find that when you reopen your database it will open to the last Dashboard layout that you had viewed. This behavior will repeat and ACT! will continue to open automatically to the Dashboard layout that you had last viewed.

> Remember, the various ACT! preferences are **machine-specific** and not **user-specific**. That means that if all of the users of your ACT! database develop Dashboard envy and decide that they too would like to have ACT! open to the Dashboard view, you'll have to wander over to each of their machines separately, to make the change.

8
Filtering Dashboards

In this chapter, we will cover:

- Filtering Contacts Dashboards
- Filtering Activity Dashboards
- Filtering Opportunity Dashboards
- Filtering Admin Dashboards
- Refreshing the Dashboard Data

Introduction

You can filter the data in each of the components in a Dashboard to determine what information will appear. Each component has different filtering options based on the types of data that component displays. For example, an opportunity component lets you filter according to the stage of your sales process, and an activity component lets you filter according to the type of tasks that you want to display.

The filter options that you set for each component are **sticky**, which means a component retains its filter settings the next time you start up ACT!. An ACT! Manager or Administrator can permanently change the filters using the Dashboard Designer. In addition, the data security rules in your database take precedence over the filters you select, which means you won't be able to see information in a Dashboard that you don't have access to.

Keep in mind that the filter settings you select are optional and based on the customizations that you have created for your database. For example, if you only have one sales process then your opportunity components will reflect only that single sales process. If you are the sole user of your database then your name is the only name that will appear when selecting the users whose information will appear in a component. And, if you have the Pro version of ACT!, you won't be able to select the names of the database users like you can in the Premium version.

Filtering the Contacts Dashboards

The following components are based on contact information:

- Recently created contacts
- Recently edited contacts

Getting ready

You'll find that the contact components will be completely empty, unless you've recently added new contacts or edited existing ones. However, if you have made changes to the contacts in your database you might want to use the Contacts Dashboard to easily track those changes.

How to do it...

1. Click the **Dashboard** icon on the navigation bar to open the Dashboard view.
2. Chose the **ACT! Contacts Dashboard** from the **Dashboard** drop-down list.
3. Click the **Filter** button on the component you want to filter data for. The **Filter Criteria** dialog box opens like the following screenshot:

4. Indicate the number of days you want to include in the component.

5. Select the Record Managers whose records you want to include in the Dashboard component or click one of the Record Manager buttons:
    - **Current User**: Selects just the name you used to log in to the database
    - **Clear All**: Removes the checkmarks next to all user names
    - **Check All**: Select the names of all the users of the database
6. Click **OK** to close the **Filter Criteria** dialog box.

How it works...

The filters determine which data will appear on the dashboard component. If you increase the number of days to include a larger date range, you'll end up with a longer list of contact records.

The Record Manager helps you to determine whose contacts you wish to track. For example, if you want to see all the contacts that were added to your database by your entire company you would select the names of all of the Record Managers. Alternatively if you wanted to measure the productivity of a single employee, you would deselect the names of all the users except for his.

There's more...

As you begin to access the various Dashboards you'll get a feeling for the amount of data that you want to see in any single component and more importantly, the kind of data that will appear.

Filtered data is limited by what you can access. If you can't access the data for a user you select, you won't see the data in the component.

A Dashboard component takes up a little less than a sixth of your computer screen. Consequently, don't try to include too much information in a component or you won't be able to see all the information in a component without having to mess with your scroll bars. For example, displaying all the opportunities for the 365 days is probably a bit of overkill.

Filtering the Activity Dashboards

Many organizations want a way to measure the productivity of their employees. Although ACT! supplies a number of reports that will show you that information, the fastest way to access that information is by looking at the Activities Dashboard which contains three activity based components:

- My Schedule At-A-Glance
- Activities by User
- Activity List

Not surprisingly, the filtering options for the activity components offer the same options that you find when scheduling an activity in the first place.

Getting ready

It makes sense that in order to **view** activities in an Activity Dashboard component, you need to have **scheduled** an activity or two in the first place.

How to do it...

1. Click the **Dashboard** icon on the navigation bar to open the Dashboard view.
2. Select the **ACT! Activities Dashboard** from the **Dashboard** drop-down list.
3. Click the **Filter** button on the component you want to filter data for. The **Filter** dialog box opens as shown in the following screenshot:

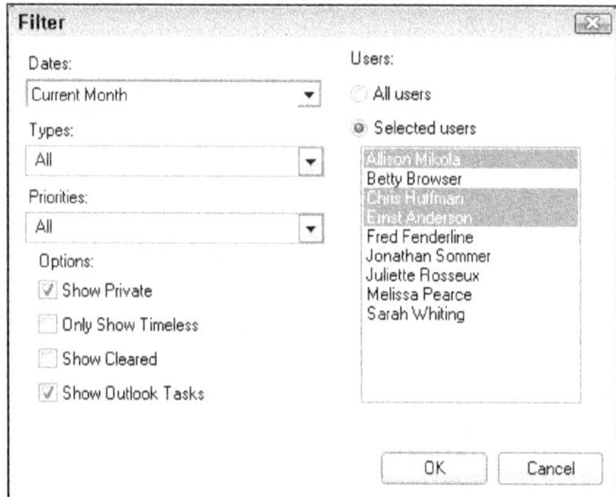

4. Select the date range you want to include in the component from the **Dates**: drop-down list.
5. Select the type of activities from the **Types**: drop-down list. You'll be happy to know that any custom activity types that you had created will appear as options in the **Types** drop-down list.
6. Select the priority of the activities from the **Priorities** drop-down list.
7. Check the options you'd like to include from the **Options** area:
    - **Show Private**: This option includes private activities as well as public ones
    - **Only Show timeless**: Shows only those activities that are not associated with a specific time of day
    - **Show Cleared**: This will include both open and cleared activities
    - **Show Outlook Tasks**: This will include Outlook and ACT! activities if you synchronize your ACT! calendar to your Outlook calendar

8. Select the users that you want to include in the component:
    - **All users**: Select this option if you want to include the activities of all the users of the database in the component
    - **Selected users**: Choose this option if you don't want to include the activities of all users and then click on the name of each user you do wish to include.
9. Click **OK** to close the **Filter Criteria** dialog box and see your changes or **Cancel** to discard your changes.

How it works...

The contents of a Dashboard component will automatically update to reflect whatever filtering criteria you chose.

There's more...

Although the activity components are fairly straightforward there are a few date variations that you may want to be aware of.

Creating a Customized Date

If you scroll all the way down to the bottom of the **Dates**: drop-down list you'll notice that **Custom...** is the last option. Just like the name implies, you can choose this option to specify a custom date range. When you select **Custom**, the calendars that you see in the following screenshot appear. Select a **From:** and a **To:** date and then click **OK** to save the date range.

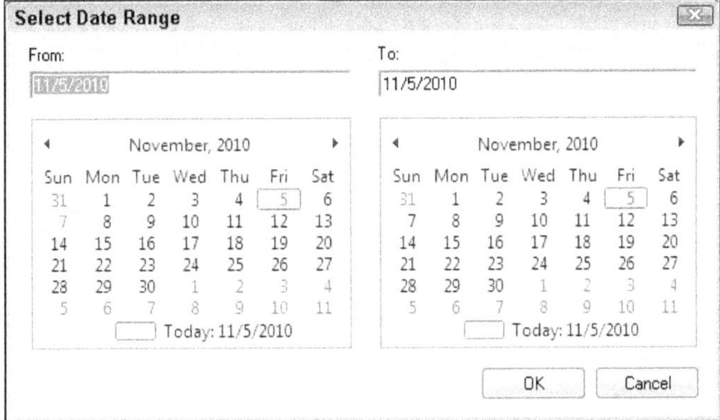

The My Schedule-At-A-Glance component works only for today's date so it doesn't offer a date option. You can see an example of the abbreviated **Filter** dialog box in the following screenshot:

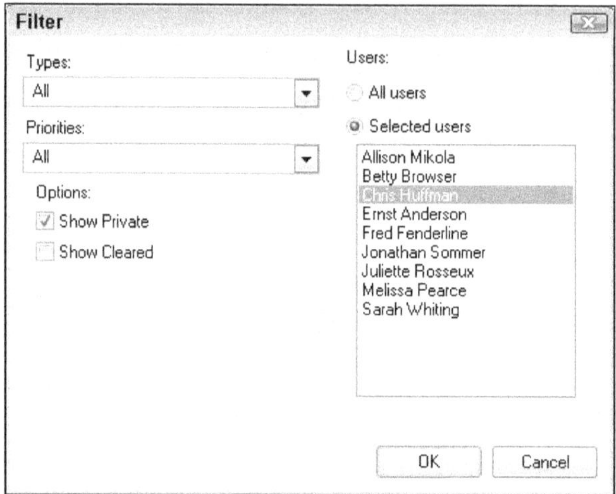

Working with the Contact History by Type component

You may consider the Contact History Count by History Type component to be somewhat of a crossover component. On the one hand, it measures history items, many of which are created when an activity is cleared. On the other hand, the filtering options are exactly the same as the ones you use when filtering contact components.

Filtering the Opportunity Dashboards

Many ACT! users love the Dashboards because they provide a visual overview of a business. Although some companies evaluate employee performance on their activities, most companies prefer to judge their employees on their ability to reach sales goals. Using the various opportunity components allows both employees and the employer to immediately see how close a sales person is to reaching their goals. In addition, the opportunity components allow the business owner to easily track the company's pipeline.

Getting ready

Needless to say, if you're going to view an opportunity component you'll want to make sure that it contains data. Therefore, you'll want to make sure that you have added a number of opportunities to your ACT! database. And, because there are a number of different opportunity components you'll want to make sure that your opportunities encompass most of your existing sales stages and include a good sampling of your company's product line.

How to do it...

1. Click the **Dashboard** icon on the navigation bar to open the Dashboard view.
2. Choose the **ACT! Opportunities Dashboard** from the **Dashboard** drop-down list.
3. Click the **Filter** button on the component you want to filter data for. The **Filter** dialog box opens like the following one:

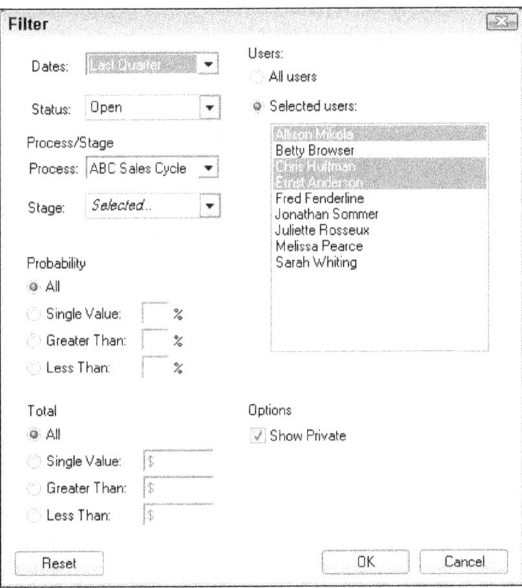

4. Select the date range you want to include in the component from the **Dates:** drop-down list.
5. Select the status of the opportunities that you want to include from the **Status**: drop-down list. You have a choice of four ACT! statuses:
   - **Open**
   - **Inactive**
   - **Closed - Won**
   - **Closed - Lost**
6. Select the process you want to track from the **Process:** drop-down list. If your database only has a single sales process then the drop-down will only show a single entry.
7. Select the stages that correspond to the **Opportunity Process** that you selected in step 6 by click the **Stage:** drop-down and select the desired stages.

8. Select the probability of closing percentage operator and fill in a percentage value in the **Probability** area.
9. Select the total value operator and fill in a dollar amount in the **Total** area.
10. Select the users whose data, you'd like to include in the component.
11. Click **Show Private** to include those opportunities that had been marked as private.
12. Click **OK** to close the **Filter Criteria** dialog box and see your changes reflected in the Dashboard component or **Cancel** to discard your changes.

How it works...

The filters you set determine the information that will appear in the component. For example, if you filter the Opportunity Pipeline by Stage component to include only those opportunities that have a better than 50 percent chance of closing and have a dollar value greater than $10,000, you'll see a much smaller pipeline than you would if you viewed simply all opportunities regardless of closing percentage or dollar amount.

There's more...

All opportunities components have the exact same filtering options. The only things that separate the various components are the filtering options they're set to and the format of the data.

Filtering the Admin Dashboard

As the name implies, the ACT! Administrative Dashboard is geared towards users who have the role of Administrator of an ACT! database.

There are three administrative components:

- User Status
- Remote Database Synch Status by User
- Remote Database information by User

The first of these components is designed to allow ACT! Administrative a way to view when the various database users log in and out of the ACT! database. The second two components only apply to those databases that have remote **synch** databases that send and receive information to and from the master database, from a remote location.

Getting ready

If you are the sole user of your ACT! Database, this section will not apply to you. However, if you have multiple users accessing your database then you might find the User Status component to be useful. And, should you have a number of remote users synching their changes back to a master database, you'll definitely want to make use of the two Dashboard components that show remote synchronization activity and database information.

How to do it...

1. Click the **Dashboard** icon on the navigation bar to open the Dashboard view.
2. Chose the **ACT! Administrative Dashboard** from the **Dashboard** drop-down list.
3. Click the **Filter** button on the **User Status** component. The **Filter** dialog box opens as shown in the following screenshot:

4. Select the users whose data you'd like to include in the component.
5. Click **OK** to close the **Filter Criteria** dialog box and see your changes reflected in the Dashboard component or **Cancel** to discard your changes.

How it works...

You will see the login information for each of your database users like the one you see in the following screenshot:

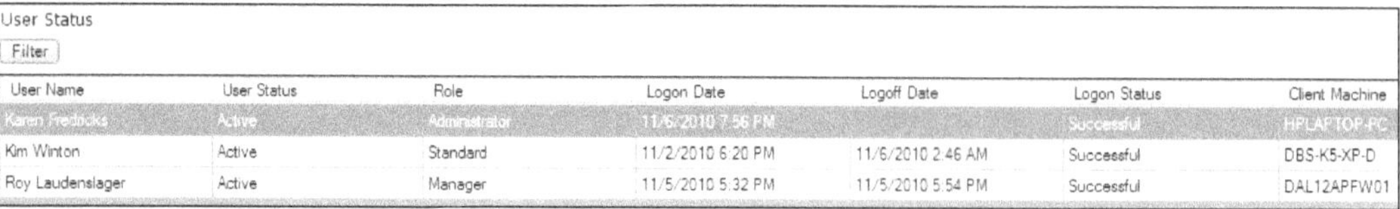

User Name	User Status	Role	Logon Date	Logoff Date	Logon Status	Client Machine
Karen Fredricks	Active	Administrator	11/6/2010 7:56 PM		Successful	HPLAPTOP-PC
Kim Winton	Active	Standard	11/2/2010 6:20 PM	11/6/2010 2:46 AM	Successful	DBS-K5-XP-D
Roy Laudenslager	Active	Manager	11/5/2010 5:32 PM	11/5/2010 5:54 PM	Successful	DAL12APFW01

There's more...

Although theoretically you can filter the Administrative components to only show information about specific users, it probably makes more sense to leave the settings set to all users so that you can have a full view of the usage of your database. It's nice to see at a glance which users are accessing the database and which ones aren't. Equally important is the ability to check on synch users to make sure that their data is being sent to the master database on a timely basis.

Changing the Dashboard Data

One of the things you might find particularly appealing about Dashboards is that you can work directly from a few of the Activity and Opportunity list view components. You might be looking at your Top 10 Opportunities and realize that you left out a very important new Opportunity; you can add it *on-the-fly* and the Dashboard component will update to reflect your change.

The options for each Dashboard component vary slightly. For example, you can schedule a new appointment from the My Schedule-At-A-Glance component or delete an Opportunity from the Top 10 Opportunities component.

Getting ready

Most of the Dashboard components aren't helpful unless they contain some data. However, because you can add information to the following components it doesn't matter if they start out empty:

- My Schedule At-A-Glance
- Activity List
- Top 10 Opportunities

How to do it...

1. Click the **Dashboard** icon on the navigation bar to open the Dashboard view.
2. Choose the **ACT! Activities**, **Default**, or **Opportunities Dashboard** from the **Dashboard** drop-down list depending on which component you want to add data to.
3. Right-click the component and choose **Schedule** if you're working from an Activity Component, or one of the Opportunity options (**New** or **Delete**) if you're working on an Opportunity component. The following screenshot shows you an example of adding data to the Top 10 Opportunities component.
4. Add the **new opportunity** or activity information.

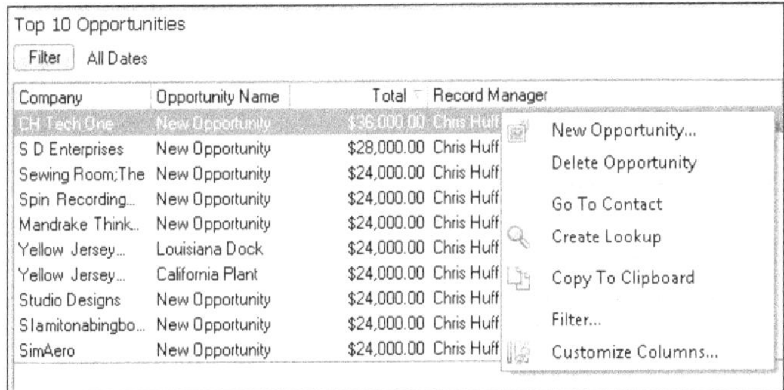

How it works...

Once you've added new, or changed existing information, it will appear in the component the next time you look.

There's more...

Returning to the Dashboard view works a bit differently, depending on the component you are working with.

Adding an Activity

When adding an **Activity** to the **My Schedule At-A-Glance** or **Activity List** components, the **Schedule Activity** dialog window will open. Once you create the new activity and click **OK** to save it you will return to the Dashboard you were looking at.

Creating a New Opportunity

Creating a new Opportunity requires its very own view rather than a dialog window that you use when creating a new activity. Therefore, when you add a new Opportunity to the Top 10 Opportunities component, you will land in the **Opportunities Detail View** where you can add all the pertinent information. Once finished, you'll need to click the **Dashboard** icon on the navigation bar to return to the Dashboard view. Luckily, you will return to the last Dashboard you were viewing.

Deleting an Opportunity

If you delete an opportunity from the Top 10 opportunities, you will receive a warning dialog box. Once you answer yes to the prompt, the opportunity will be removed from your database and you'll be returned to the Dashboard you were previously viewing; you'll notice that the opportunity you deleted will no longer appear.

9
Editing Existing Dashboards

In this chapter, we will cover:

- Cloning an existing Dashboard
- Changing the Dashboard display type
- Changing the Dashboard default filters
- Changing the Dashboard headers and footers
- Changing the Dashboard legends
- Changing the Dashboard totals
- Changing the Dashboard scales and limits
- Setting a Dashboard target
- Modifying the closed sales to date component
- Changing data chart properties

Introduction

ACT! users with Manager or Administrator privileges can use the Dashboard designer to edit existing Dashboards or to create new ones. This chapter focuses on taking the **out of the box** Dashboards and making them your own. For example, you might decide that you would like to view the Activities by User component as a list display, or you may want to change the Opportunity Pipeline by Stage filters to reflect the member of your sales force on a permanent basis so that you don't have to change it every time you access it.

Cloning an existing Dashboard

You can create a new Dashboard layout from scratch if you have an abundance of time and energy on your hands. However, you will probably find it a whole lot easier to save one of the default Dashboards under a new name and then start the tweaking process. This method is not only a whole lot easier than starting from scratch it's also a whole lot safer; if you manage to mangle a Dashboard beyond use you can always start back at square one!

Getting ready

The first thing you need to do is decide exactly what data you want to appear in your new Dashboard. For example, you might be a Sales Manager and decide that you want to have a separate Dashboard for each member of your sales team; in that case the ACT! default Dashboard might be a good starting place. Or maybe you would like to see total sales and opportunities for your entire company and not just one individual; in that case the ACT! Opportunities Dashboard would be a good place to start.

How to do it...

1. Click the **Dashboard** icon on the navigation bar to open the Dashboard view.
2. Choose the Dashboard you want to clone from the **Dashboard** drop-down list.
3. Click the **Edit Current Dashboard** icon in the Dashboard menu bar. The Dashboard designer that you see in the following screenshot will open:

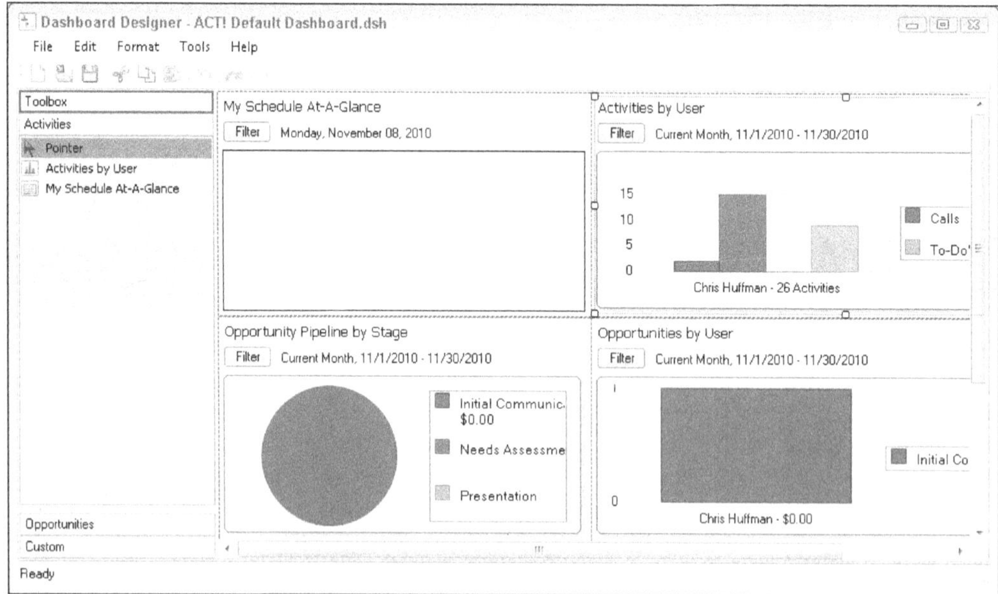

4. Click **File** and Choose **Save As...**. This will prompt the **Save As** dialog box to open.
5. Enter the name of the new Dashboard in the **File Name** box and then click **Save**.
6. Click **File** and choose **Exit** to close the Dashboard.

How it works...

Once you have cloned a Dashboard it will appear in the list of Dashboards in the Dashboard drop-down list.

There's more...

ACT! assigns all Dashboards the `.dsh` extension and saves the Dashboards in the Dashboards sub-folder of your database.

Changing the Dashboard display type

If variety is the spice of life then ACT! must be highly seasoned. ACT! comes with a variety of different Dashboard component display types, which means you can see the same information in a number of ways.

The following screenshot shows you the five basic component display types:

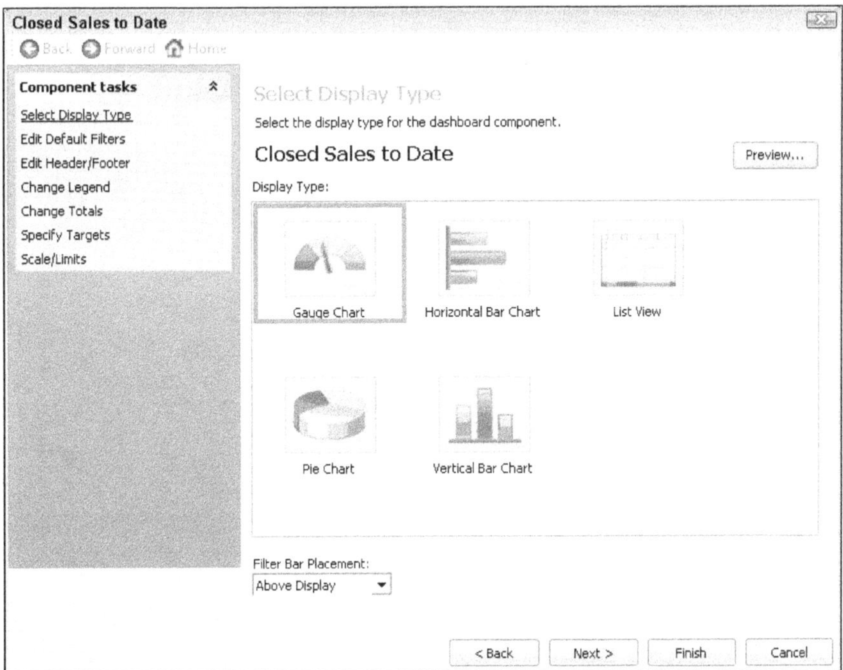

Not all display types can be used with all components. For example, the **Closed Sales to Date** component can be configured with any of the display types, whereas the **Top 10 Opportunities** component can only be viewed in **List View**. In addition, some components such as the **My Schedule At-A-Glance** use the **Calendar View** which can't be used with other components.

Getting ready

It seems kind of obvious that in order to change something you'll need to have first identified what exactly it is that needs changing. As this section works with Display Types we'll make the assumption that you've already identified a component that you would like to see displayed in a different fashion.

How to do it...

1. Click on the **Dashboard** icon on the navigation bar to access the Dashboard view.
2. Select the Dashboard you want to modify from the **Dashboard** drop-down list and then click the **Edit** button on the Dashboard tool bar. The Dashboard designer opens.
3. Right-click on the component that you would like to change and select **Component Configuration** from the contextual menu; alternatively you can double-click the component. In either event, the **Component Configuration** wizard magically appears similar to the one you see in the following screenshot:

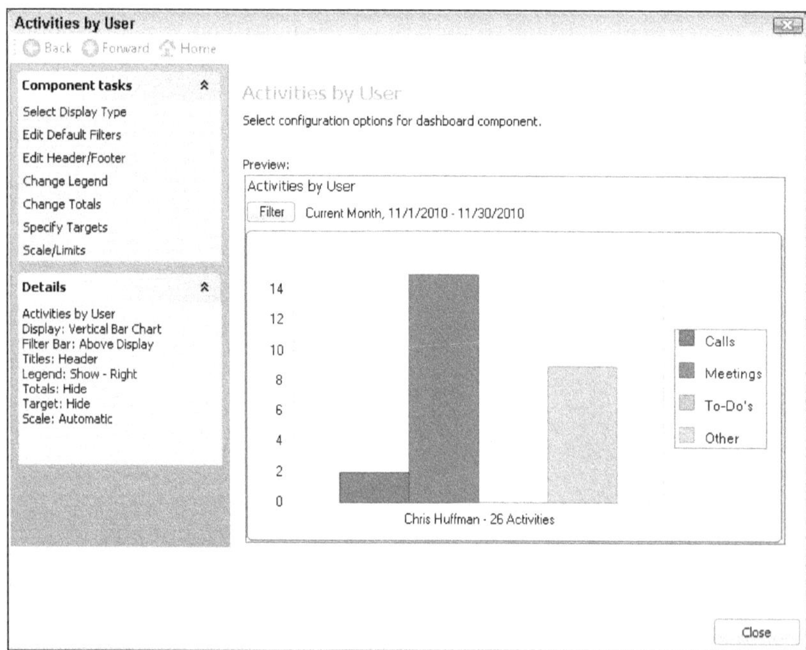

4. Click **Select Display Type** from the **Component Tasks** area of the **Component Configuration** wizard, and click the **Display Type** that you would like to use.
5. Click **Preview** to review your changes in the **Dashboard Component Preview** window and then click **Close** to close it.
6. Click **Finish** when you are done working with the **Component Tasks** and then **Yes** to the dialog box to save your changes to the component.
7. Click **Close** to close the Dashboard designer and then **Yes** to save the changes to the Dashboard.

How it works...

Your data will now display in the **Display Type** format that you chose.

See also

There is a saying–*if it's not broken, don't fix it*. That adage holds true for the Dashboards. Rather than make a permanent change to an existing Dashboard consider saving that Dashboard with a different name just in case you prefer the original components to your new **improved** versions. For a refresher in saving a Dashboard read the Cloning an Existing Dashboard section earlier in this chapter.

Changing the Dashboard default filters

If you find yourself heading to the Filter button every time you look at a Dashboard Component, it's time to think about changing them on a permanent basis. For me, changing the filters for a Dashboard Component is one of the most logical changes you can make. After all, it doesn't make a lot of sense to view old Opportunities, or look at the activities of someone who is no longer with your company.

Getting ready

Getting ready for this recipe is easy: if you're constantly filtering a Dashboard then it's time for a change!

How to do it...

1. Click the **Dashboard** icon on the navigation bar to access the Dashboard view.
2. Select the Dashboard you want to modify from the **Dashboard** drop-down list and then click the **Edit** button on the Dashboard tool bar. The Dashboard designer opens.

3. Right-click on the component that you would like to change and select **Component Configuration** from the contextual menu; alternatively you can double-click the component. In either event, the Component Configuration wizard appears.
4. Click **Edit Default Filters** from the **Component Tasks** area of the **Component Configuration** wizard. The **Edit Default Filters** dialog window will open similar to the one you see in the following screenshot:

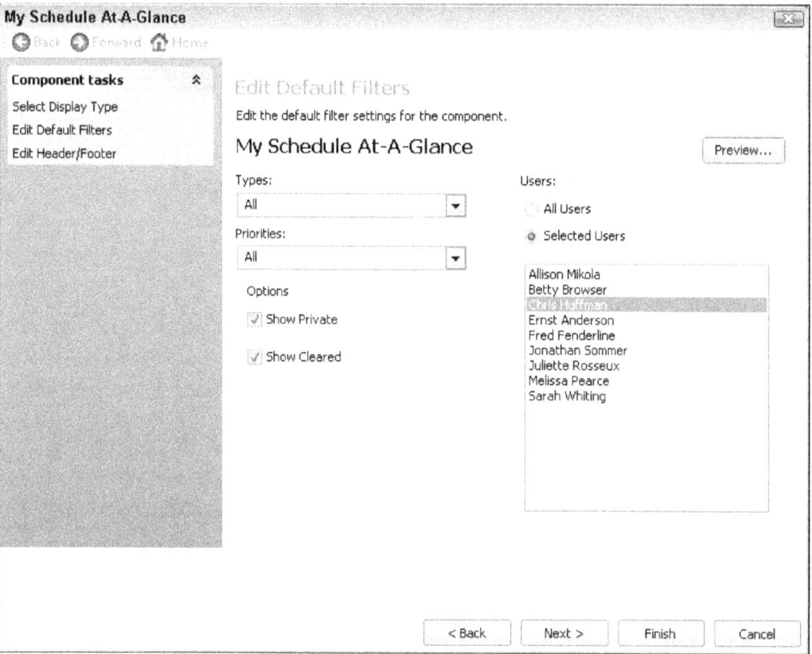

5. Make any filtering changes that you need.
6. Click **Preview** to review your changes in the **Dashboard Component Preview** window and then click **Close** to close the preview.
7. Click **Finish** when you are done working with the **Component Task**s and then **Yes** to the dialog box to save your changes to the component.
8. Click **Close** to close the Dashboard designer and then **Yes** to save the changes to the Dashboard.

How it works...

Because Dashboard components measure various types of information it's only logical that the various components contain different filtering options.

There's more...

Whatever filtering options you see when filtering a Dashboard component will also be available when you edit the filters in the Component Configuration wizard. However, although any changes you make from the Dashboard view will have to be repeated the next time you access a Dashboard, changes you make in the Dashboard designer are permanent.

Changes that a Manager or Administrator makes to the filters for a component in the Dashboard designer change the default filters for all users. However, users can continue to change the filters for their own purposes directly from Dashboard; those changes just won't be permanent.

Changing the Dashboard headers and footers

You've just got to love a software program that is as flexible as ACT!. By now you should be really comfortable about making changes to the ACT! Dashboards and their components. Changing a component's headers and footers is a great way to describe exactly what a Dashboard component does. For example, you might have changed the default Opportunity by User component to reflect just those individuals in one specific sales team; changing the header makes looking at the component a whole lot clearer.

Getting ready

By now you know the drill; in order to **change** a component you need to first identify the component that **needs** changing.

How to do it...

1. Click the **Dashboard** icon on the navigation bar to access the Dashboard view.
2. Select the Dashboard you want to modify from the **Dashboard** drop-down list and then click the **Edit** button on the Dashboard toolbar. The Dashboard designer opens.
3. Right-click on the component that you would like to change and select **Component Configuration** from the contextual menu; the **Component Configuration** wizard appears.

4. Click **Edit Header/Footer** from the **Component Tasks** area of the **Component Configuration** wizard. The **Edit Header/Footer** dialog window will open similar to the one you see in the following screenshot:

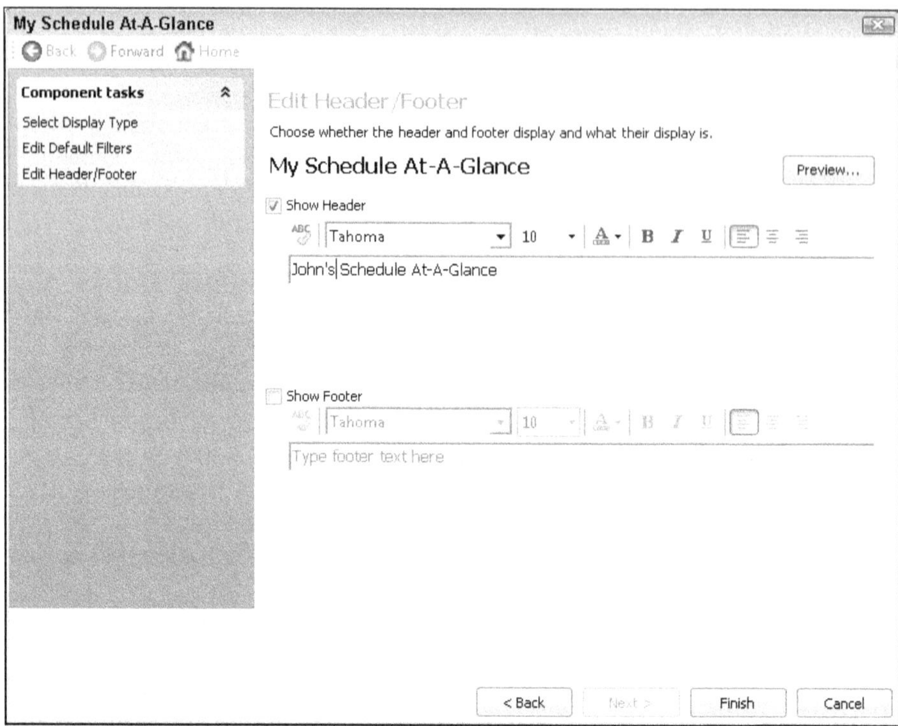

5. To change an existing header:
   i. Place a checkmark in the **Show Header** checkbox to include a header
   ii. Select a font, size, and other formatting attributes
   iii. Fill in the header information
6. To add a footer:
   i. Place a checkmark in the Show Footer checkbox to include a Footer
   ii. Select a font, size, and other formatting attributes
   iii. Fill in the footer information
7. Click **Preview** to review your changes in the **Dashboard Component Preview** window and then click **Close** to close the preview.
8. Click **Finish** when you are done working with the **Component Tasks** and then **Yes** to the dialog box to save your changes to the component.
9. Click **Close** to close the Dashboard designer and then **Yes** to save the changes to the Dashboard.

How it works...

In essence, a Dashboard component's header labels the component.

There's more...

Most of the component headers are fairly generic and can apply to almost any filtering options you select. However, when you move on to creating new Dashboards from scratch you'll really see the importance of changing the component headers. For example, you might create a new Sales Dashboard that will include a separate component for each of your sales people. Changing the header of each component to reflect the sales person's name will make the Dashboard a whole lot easier to understand!

As an author, my function should be to disseminate information and not critique it. However, in the case of the component footers, it makes you wonder if Sage ever actually took a look at them. This is not because none of the **out of the box** Dashboards include footers. Or maybe Sage didn't include them because they realized they don't work very well.

The following screenshot shows you a footer, and how it blends into the header of the component right below it:

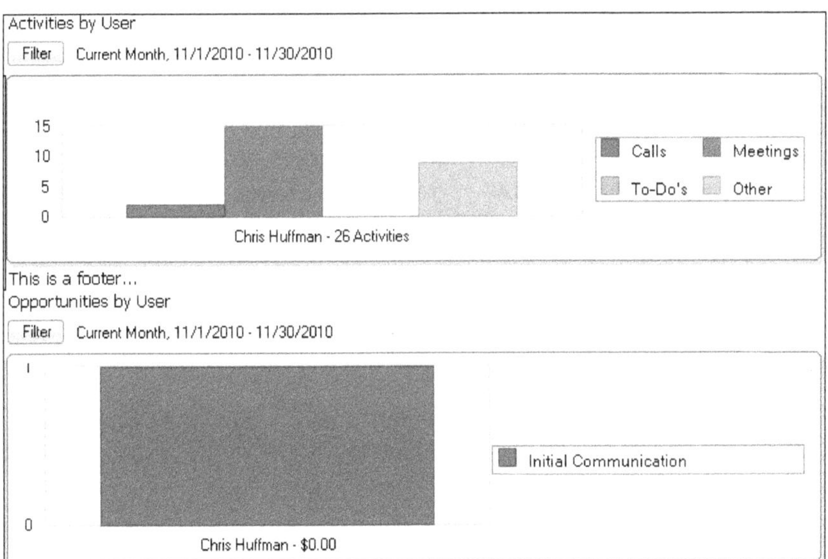

Changing the Dashboard legends

Each graphical Dashboard component comes with a legend that explains the conventions used in the component. Unfortunately there isn't much you can do to change those legends except to move them around to different areas of the component.

Getting ready

The first thing you'll want to do is identify the component that you feel needs a legend relocation. By default, all the legends reside on the right-side of the component like the one you see in the following screenshot:

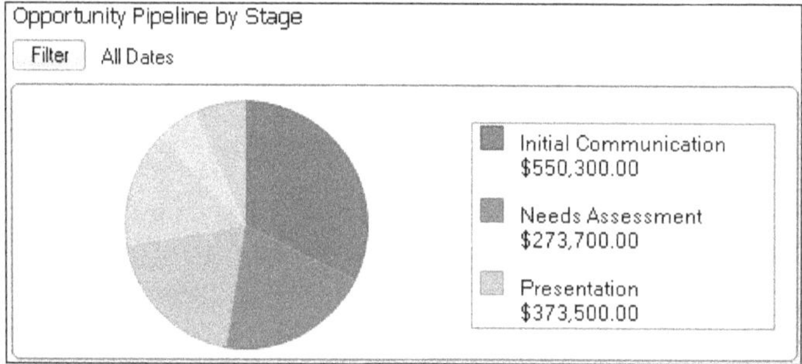

How to do it...

1. Click the **Dashboard** icon on the navigation bar to access the Dashboard view.
2. Select the Dashboard you want to modify from the **Dashboard** drop-down list and then click the **Edit** button on the Dashboard tool bar. The Dashboard designer opens.
3. Right-click on the component that you'd like to change and select **Component Configuration** from the contextual menu; the **Component Configuration** wizard appears.
4. Click **Change Legend** from the **Component Tasks** area of the **Component Configuration** wizard. The **Change Legend** dialog window will open similar to the one you see in the following screenshot:

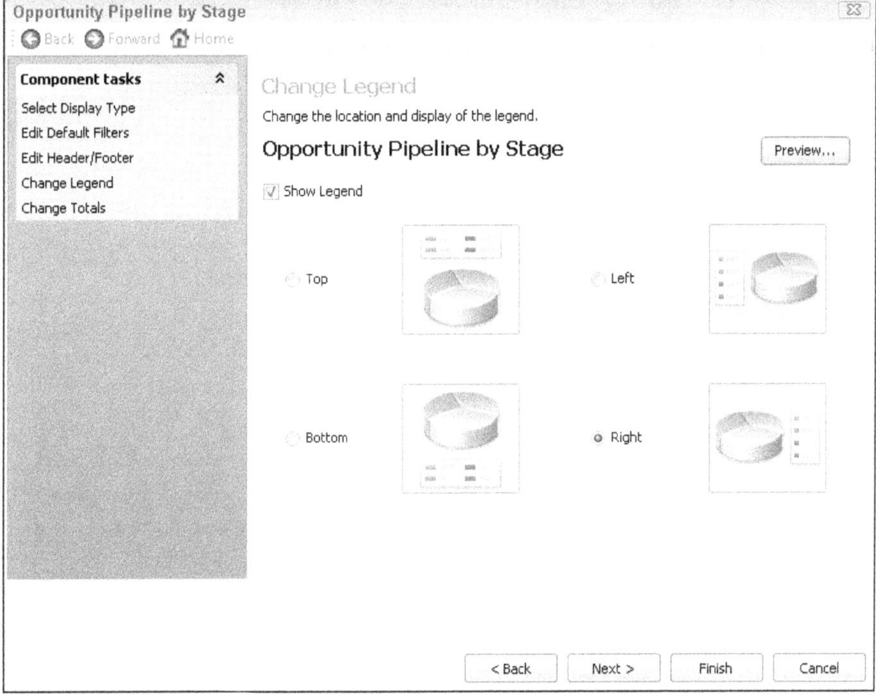

5. Select the new legend location (**Top**, **Bottom**, **Left**, or **Right**).
6. Click **Preview** to review your changes in the **Dashboard Component Preview** window and then click **Close** to close the preview.
7. Click **Finish** when you are done working with the **Component Tasks** and then **Yes** to the dialog box to save your changes to the component.
8. Click **Close** to close the Dashboard designer and then **Yes** to save the changes to the Dashboard.

How it works...

The legend will now appear in the location that you indicated.

There's more...

If for whatever reason you would prefer not to have a legend, you can remove the legend by removing the checkmark in the **Show Legend** option in the **Change Legend** dialog window.

Changing the Dashboard totals

Although a picture may be worth a thousand words, sometimes a few words might greatly enhance the meaning of a picture—especially in the case of a Dashboard component graph or chart. The following screenshot shows you the **Activities by User** component without totals:

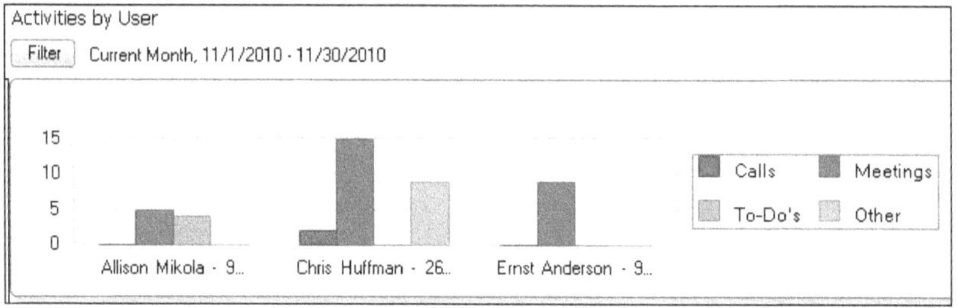

Although the chart gives us a good sense of the activities of the various users it doesn't give us a feel for the combined effort of the three sales people. The following screenshot shows you the same component with the addition of totals:

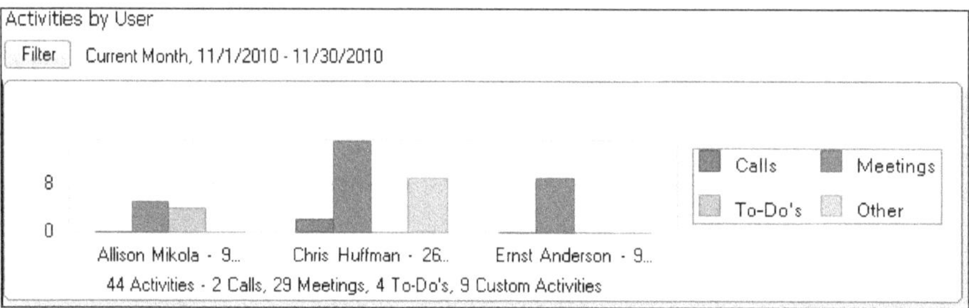

How to do it...

1. Click the **Dashboard** icon on the navigation bar to access the Dashboard view.
2. Select the Dashboard you want to modify from the **Dashboard** drop-down list and then click the **Edit** button on the Dashboard tool bar. The Dashboard designer opens.
3. Right-click on the component that you would like to change and select **Component Configuration** from the contextual menu; the **Component Configuration** wizard appears.
4. Click **Change Totals** from the **Component Tasks** area of the **Component Configuration** wizard. The **Change Totals** dialog window will open similar to the one you see in the following screenshot:

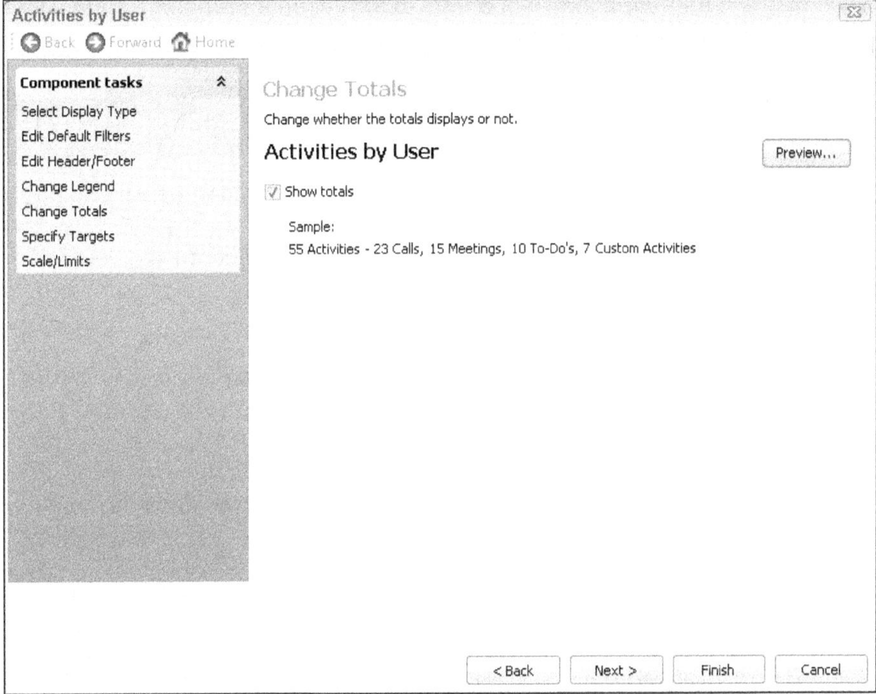

5. Place a checkmark in the **Show totals** checkbox.
6. Click **Preview** to review your changes in the **Dashboard Component Preview** window and then click **Close** to close the preview.
7. Click **Finish** when you are done working with the **Component Tasks** and then **Yes** to the dialog box to save your changes to the component.
8. Click **Close** to close the Dashboard designer and then **Yes** to save the changes to the Dashboard.

How it works...

A recap of the component will now appear at the bottom of the component.

There's more...

By default, most of the components do not display totals. In addition, you can't add totals to any of the components that use the list display.

As you change the filters on a component to which you have added a total, the total will automatically update to reflect the filtering changes.

Although you may find that the addition of a total to a component is helpful, unfortunately there are no other component options other than the ability to either turn them on or off.

Changing the Dashboard scales and limits

Editing the scales and limits on the Dashboard components is a **good news, bad news** type of feature. The good news is that you can easily change these items; the bad news is that knowing which components contains scales or limits can be a bit confusing. And, once you determine which components contain scales or limits, you have to do a bit of mental math to come up with the proper values.

A **scale** is the interval unit used in a bar chart. For example, depending on the products you sell, you might measure your sales pipeline in intervals of hundreds, thousands, or even billions. Like its name implies a **limit** *limits* the amount of data that you see in a component. For example, by default the top 10 opportunities component limits the data to 10 items. However, you can change that limit to only include fewer items or increase the limit to include more than 10 items.

Getting ready

You will want to take a logical look at the various Dashboard components to decide in advance which ones have scales or limits that you can change. A good rule of thumb is that you can change the scales or limits of components that display their information in a vertical bar chart. If a component is in the shape of a pie chart, you won't be able to change the scales or limits. In the case of the top opportunities component, you will be able to change the *limit* but not the *scale*.

How to do it...

1. Click the **Dashboard** icon on the navigation bar to access the Dashboard view.
2. Select the Dashboard you want to modify from the **Dashboard** drop-down list and then click the **Edit** button on the Dashboard tool bar. The Dashboard designer opens.
3. Right-click on the component that you'd like to change and select **Component Configuration** from the contextual menu; the **Component Configuration** wizard appears.
4. Click **Scale/Limits** from the **Component Tasks** area of the **Component Configuration** wizard. The **Scales/Limits** dialog window will open similar to the one you see in the following screenshot:

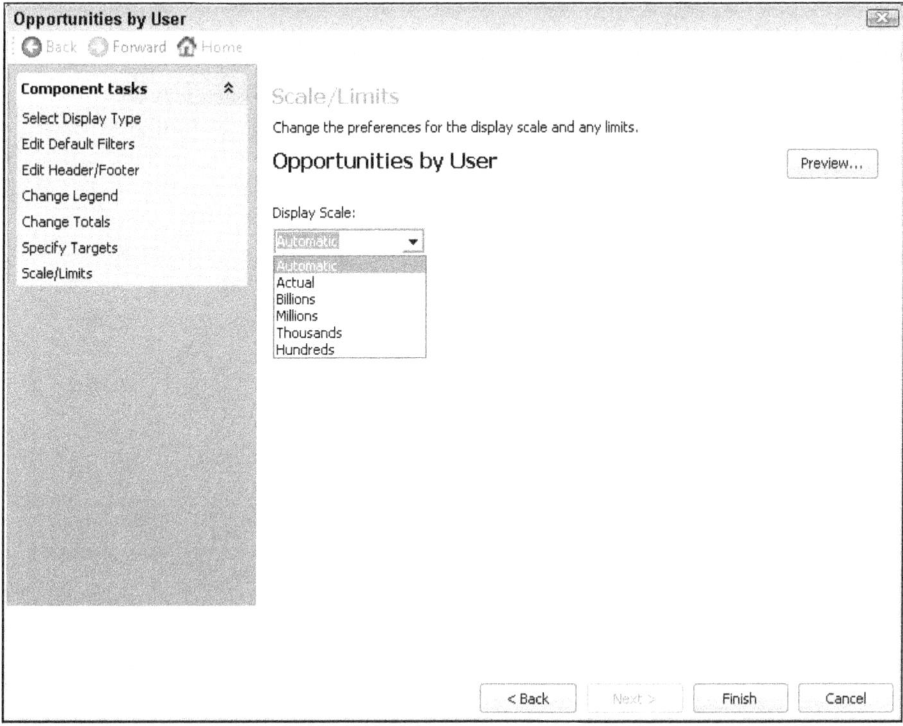

5. Select a scale from the **Display Scale** drop-down.
6. Click **Preview...** to review your changes in the **Dashboard Component Preview** window and then click **Close** to close the preview.
7. Click **Finish** when you are done working with the **Component Tasks** and then **Yes** to the dialog box to save your changes to the component.
8. Click **Close** to close the Dashboard designer and then **Yes** to save the changes to the Dashboard.

How it works...

The component data will now reflect the scale criteria that you indicated in step 5 shown previously. You will want to make sure that the scale you indicated reflects the type of data that will appear in the component. For example, if your typical sales are measured in the hundreds then choosing billions as the scale won't make a lot of sense unless you sell literally billions of your products.

There's more...

You can change either the scale or limit on a component but not both. The following screenshot shows you an example of the top 10 opportunities in the **Component Configuration** wizard. You get there by following the exact same steps outlined previously; however, that particular component allows you to change the limits rather than the scale.

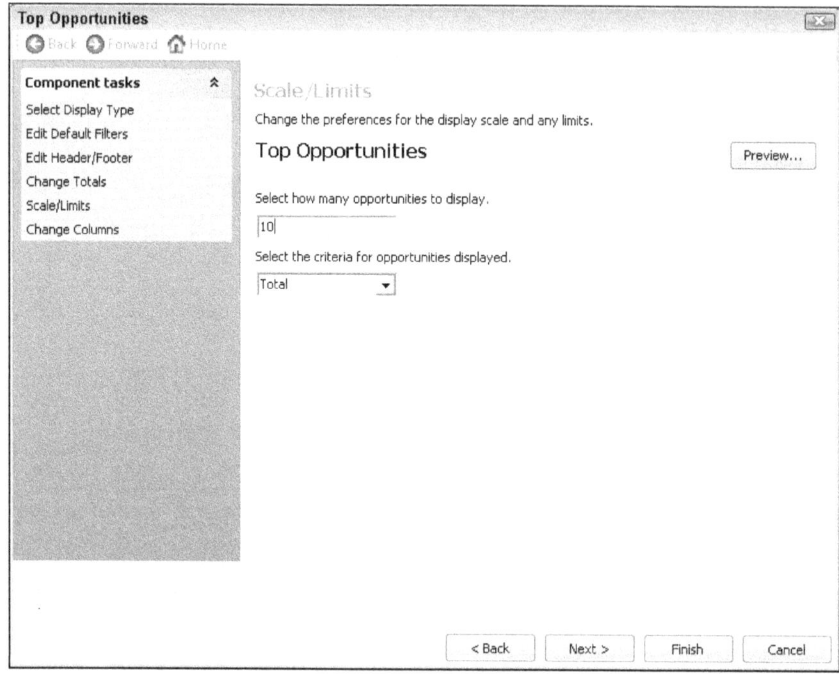

See also

If you change the scaling on a Dashboard component, you may consider editing the component's header or footer to indicate the parameters you used. Changing the Dashboard headers and footers is a great way to provide this information; you may want to view the *Changing the Dashboard headers and footers* section above if you are not sure how to change that information.

Setting a Dashboard target

In ACT!, there are two easy ways to measure performance; one way is to measure the activities of a user and the other is to measure the opportunities of a user. This information can be garnered through the use of the various ACT! Reports; however, the reports don't reflect how close a user comes to actually reaching a goal set by management.

Several of the Dashboard components allow you to measure how close users come to reaching their goals by allowing you to set a **target**. Quite simply, a target is simply an indicator that lets you know how close you are to reaching your goal.

Getting ready

You'll find this component located on both the ACT! opportunities and the ACT! default Dashboards.

How to do it...

1. Click the **Dashboard** icon on the navigation bar to access the Dashboard view.
2. Select the Dashboard you want to modify from the **Dashboard** drop-down list and then click the **Edit** button on the Dashboard tool bar. The Dashboard designer opens.
3. Right-click on the component that you would like to change and select **Component Configuration** from the contextual menu; the **Component Configuration** wizard appears.
4. Click **Specify Targets** from the **Component Tasks** area of the **Component Configuration** wizard. The **Specify Target** dialog window will open similar to the one you see in the following screenshot:

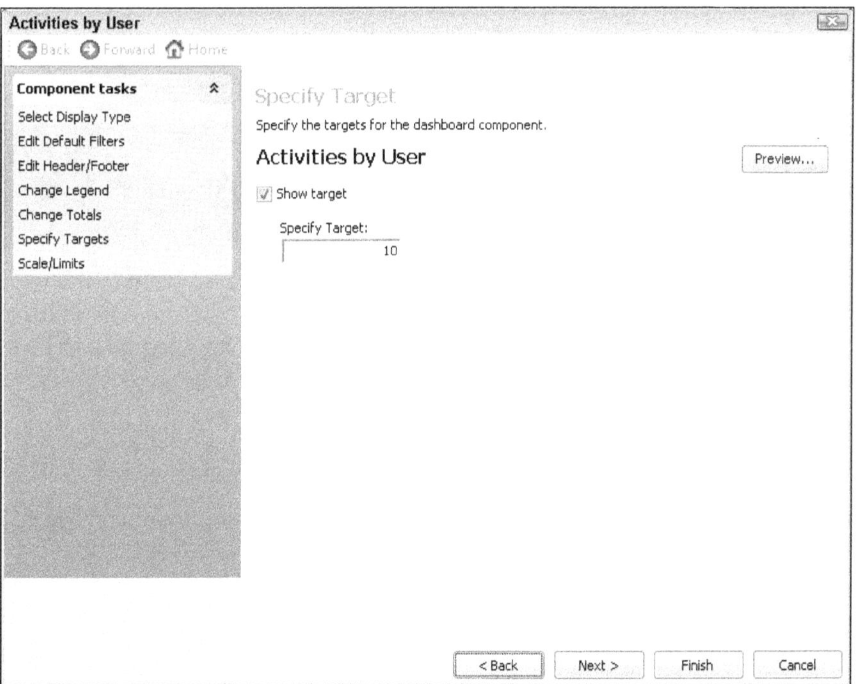

5. Place a checkmark in the **Show target** box.
6. Fill in the target value in the **Specify Target** field.
7. Click **Preview** to preview your changes in the **Dashboard Component Preview** window and then click **Close** to close the preview.
8. Click **Finish** when you are done working with the **Component Tasks** and then **Yes** to the dialog box to save your changes to the component.
9. Click **Close** to close the Dashboard designer and then **Yes** to save the changes to the Dashboard.

How it works...

The following screenshot shows you an example of a component that includes a target:

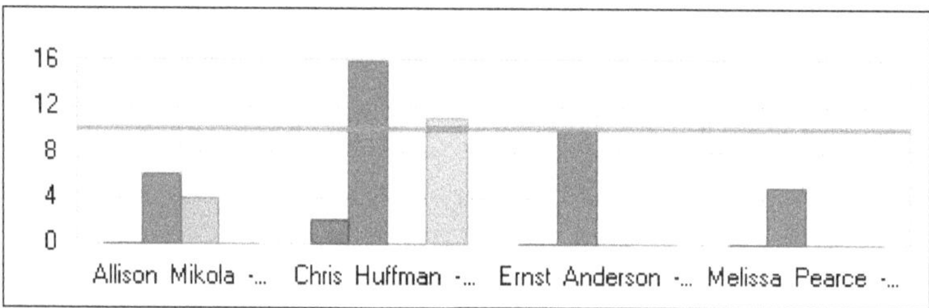

As you can see from the illustration the target appears as a horizontal line across the component making it easy to see who has met or exceeded the set goal.

Modifying the closed sales to date component

If you are managing a sales team—or if you are goal-oriented, you will want to make use of the closed sales to date component. This component offers a bit more customization opportunities than the other components. You can add a specific target goal and even include **breakpoint** or milestones that will visually show you how close you are to achieving your goal.

Getting ready

You will find the **Activities by User** and **Opportunities by User** components on the ACT! default Dashboard. Both components are ideal candidates for targets.

How to do it...

1. Click the **Dashboard** icon on the navigation bar to access the Dashboard view.
2. Select the Dashboard you want to modify from the **Dashboard** drop-down list and then click the **Edit** button on the Dashboard tool bar. The Dashboard designer opens.
3. Right-click on the component that you would like to change and select **Component Configuration** from the contextual menu; the **Component Configuration** wizard appears.
4. Click **Specify Targets** from the **Component Tasks** area of the **Component Configuration** wizard. The **Specify Target** dialog window will open.
5. Place a checkmark in the **Show Target** checkbox and fill in a target in the **Specify Target:** field.
6. Click **Preview** to review your changes in the **Dashboard Component Preview** window and then click **Close** to close the preview. As you can see in the following screenshot, this step places an indicator arrow on the component:

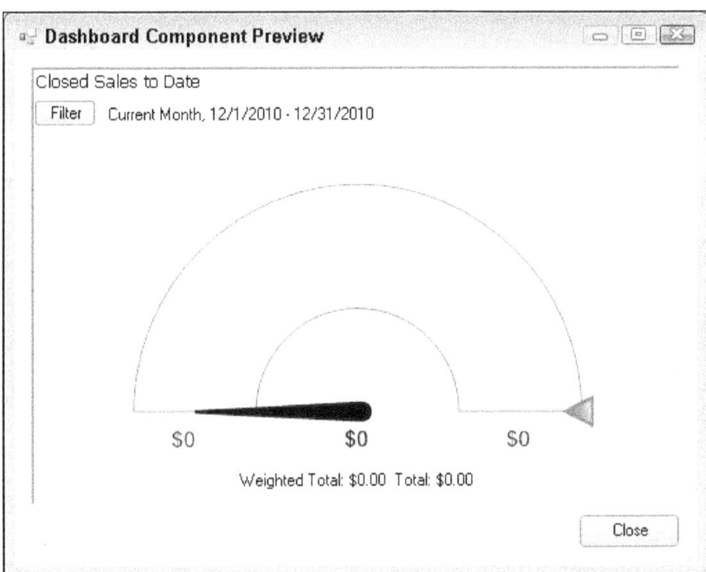

7. Click **Scales/Limits** from the **Component Tasks** area of the **Component Configuration** wizard. The **Specify Target** dialog window will open which looks like the following screenshot:

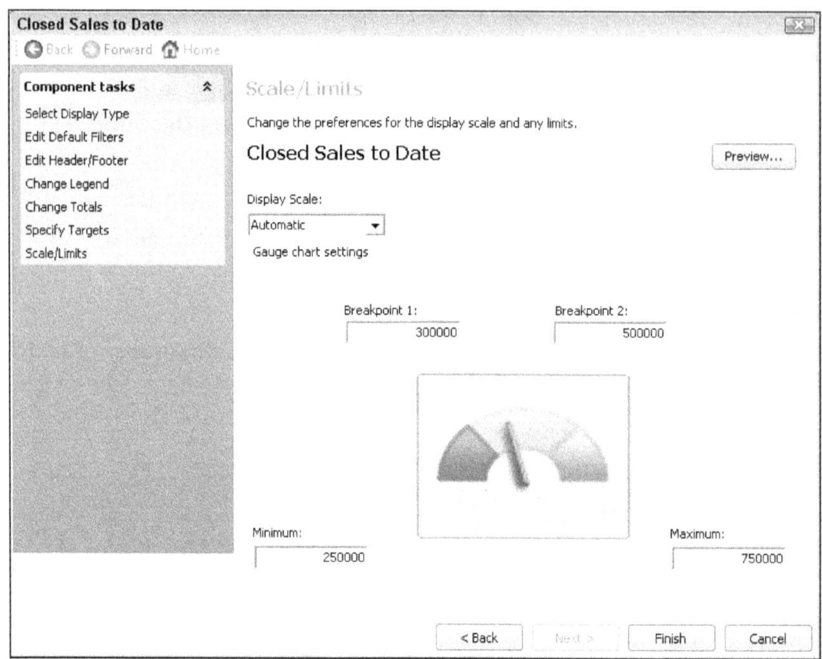

8. Specify the following elements for the component:
    - **Display Scale**: You can leave this on automatic, or specify a scale in the hundreds, thousands, millions, or billions.
    - **Breakpoint 1** and **Breakpoint 2**: These are optional but a good way to indicate milestones towards reaching your final goal.
    - **Minimum**: This indicates the smallest total amount that the component will report.
    - **Maximum**: This indicates the largest total amount that the component will report.
9. Click **Preview** to review your changes in the **Dashboard Component Preview** window and then click **Close** to close the preview. The following screenshot shows you how the breakpoints, targets, and maximum values appear on the component:

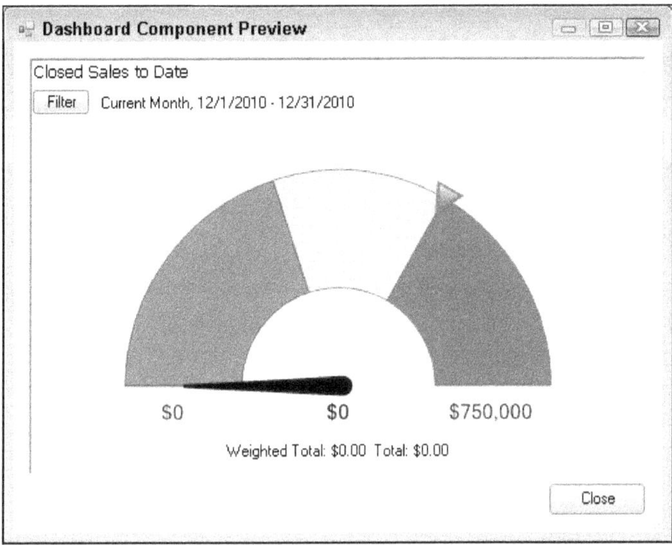

10. Click **Finish** when you are done working with the **Component Tasks** and then **Yes** to the dialog box to save your changes to the component.
11. Click **Close** to close the Dashboard designer and then **Yes** to save the changes to the Dashboard.

How it works...

Any changes you made to the targets, scales, or limits are now reflected in the closed sales to date component.

There's more...

The nice thing about ACT! is that once you have honed your skills in one area, you can apply that knowledge to many other areas of ACT!. A case in point is the closed sales to date component. Because the closed sales to date is such a versatile component you may consider cloning it for a variety of purposes and using the various recipes in this chapter to refine it. For example, you may create a component showing the total open sales for the entire sales team and title it **Open Ops** or create several components for each member of your sales team showing their monthly, quarterly, and yearly goals.

Changing the Dashboard data charts

Creating custom Dashboard components that are based on a company's unique situation requires the use of advanced SQL tools and programming skills and is beyond the scope of this book. However, the latest versions of ACT! include a number of **data charts.** Quite simply, a data chart queries a portion of a database and presents the information in the form of a Dashboard component.

Although the data charts look like the Dashboard components that you are already familiar with, there is one important distinction. Components based on a data chart can't be modified through the **Component Configuration** wizard; each component actually has its own **Chart Designer**. That means that when you make permanent changes to a data chart you will follow a slightly different procedure than the one you followed when changing the more traditional Dashboard components.

Getting ready

At the time of this writing, there are 10 data charts that you can use to create a Dashboard component.

Three of the data charts are included on the Administrative Dashboard:

- User Status
- Remote Database Synch Status
- Remote Database Information by User

An additional three data charts appear on the Contacts Dashboard:

- Recently Created Contacts
- Recently Edited Contacts
- Contact History Count by History type

There are even four data charts that don't appear on any of the Dashboards although you can add them to any of the Dashboards that you want:

- Opportunities with Contact Information
- Opportunities with Products
- Opportunity Weighted Total by Stage
- Contacts by Country

How to do it...

1. Click the **Dashboard** icon on the navigation bar to access the Dashboard view.
2. Select the Dashboard you want to modify from the **Dashboard** drop-down list and then click the **Edit** button on the Dashboard tool bar. The Dashboard designer opens.
3. Right-click on the component that you would like to change and select **Component Configuration** from the contextual menu; the **Data Chart Designer** appears. You can see what it looks like in the following screenshot:

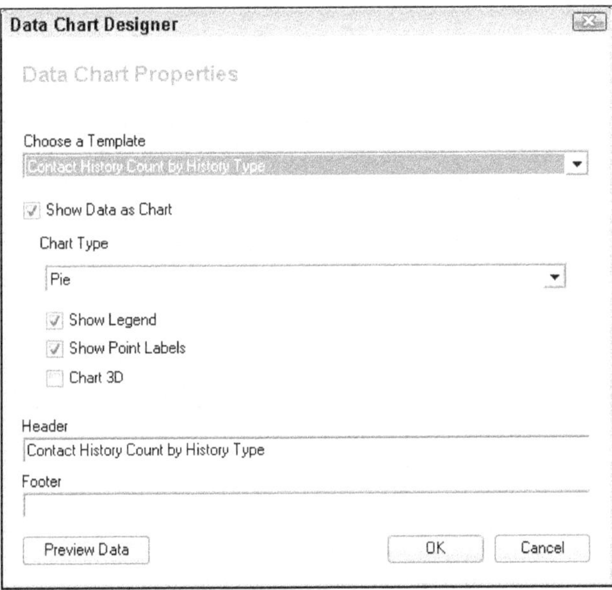

4. Select a data chart template from the **Choose a Template** drop-down list.
5. Place a checkmark in the **Show Data as Chart** checkbox if you would like to have the data to appear in the form of a chart rather than a list.
6. Select a chart type from the **Chart Type** drop-down list.
7. Place a checkmark in the **Show Legend** checkbox if you would like to include a legend for the data chart.
8. Place a checkmark in the **Show Point Labels** checkbox if you would like identify each part of the data chart.
9. Place a checkmark in the **Chart 3D** checkbox if you would like to have the data appear with a slight shadow giving the graphic a bit more depth.
10. Add a header for the data chart in the **Header** field.
11. Add a footer for the data chart in the **Footer** field.

12. Click **OK** when you are done working with the **Data Chart Designer**.
13. Click **Close** to close the Dashboard designer and then **Yes** to save the changes to the Dashboard.

There's more...

As mentioned earlier, although data charts *look* like other Dashboard components they do *work* a bit differently.

Many of the data charts have very little flexibility other than the ability to edit the header and footer information. For example, if you try to edit the **Recently Created Contacts Data Chart**, you will notice that most of the options are grayed out.

Because the data charts don't make use of the **Component Configuration** wizard, you will notice that a few useful features are missing. For example, you also can't permanently change the filters for a data chart.

You can't preview the changes you make to a data chart as you make them; however, you can move the **Data Chart Designer** window out of the way to see the effect of your changes on the data chart itself. You will also notice a **Preview Data** button; clicking that will allow you to temporarily make changes to your filters so that you can see those changes on the data chart.

One interesting data chart area that you may want to explore is the various chart types. In addition to the chart types used by the basic components, data charts can be configured in the shape of a pyramid, doughnut, or line graph.

10
Working with the Dashboard Designer

In this chapter, we will cover:

- Creating a new Dashboard
- Adding or removing columns or rows
- Creating a wider component
- Adding components to a Dashboard
- Adding custom data charts
- Rearranging the order of the Dashboards

Introduction

In previous chapters, you learned how to take the existing Dashboards that come with ACT! and make them your own. Once you feel really comfortable with both the existing Dashboards and the editing process you may want to move on and start creating your own Dashboards from scratch.

Using the ACT! Dashboard designer, you can create new Dashboards that best suit how you and your business work. ACT! users that have manager or administrator rights have the ability to add, remove, resize, and *drag-and-drop* components. They can add headers and footers and set the default filters. And, because there is no limit to the number of Dashboards that can be used in a database, they can create separate Dashboards for the various parts of a business that they want to track.

Creating a new Dashboard

Although ACT! comes with several Dashboards right out of the box you might want to create your own Dashboard that contains the specific components that you want to view. For example, you may create unique Dashboards for each member of your sales staff to show you the specifics about their individual sales and activities. Alternatively, you may create a new sales Dashboard and have each component show the sales of a specific sales person.

Getting ready

You may believe in that old adage *look before you leap* and that is definitely the case when it comes to creating new Dashboards. After all, why reinvent the wheel if the existing one works just fine? You'll want to clearly define a reporting need and make sure that one of the existing Dashboards doesn't already fulfill it.

How to do it...

1. Click the Dashboard icon on the navigation bar to access the Dashboard view.
2. Click the **Edit Current Dashboard button** on the Dashboard tool bar. The **Dashboard Designer** opens.
3. Click **File** and then choose **New** on the Dashboard Designer menu bar. An empty Dashboard like the one you see in the following screenshot appears:

4. Click **File** and then choose **Save As...** on the Dashboard Designer menu bar. The **Save As** dialog box will appear.
5. Give the Dashboard a name and then click **Save**.
6. Click **File** and choose **Exit** to close the Dashboard Designer.

How it works...

You'll now be able to select the name of your newly created Dashboard from the Dashboard drop-down in the Dashboard view.

There's more...

You may think it a bit puzzling that you need to open an existing Dashboard in order to create a new one. In several previous versions of ACT!, a new Dashboard button appeared in the toolbar of the Dashboard view. The button went AWOL in the latest versions but hopefully may reappear sometime in the future.

Adding or removing columns and rows

A new Dashboard consists of six **cells** or blank components arranged in three rows of two columns. That's a great starting place for most of us but there may be times when you want to include another row of components. For example, you might be creating a Dashboard to track the sales of each of your eight sales people and want to create a separate component for each one.

Getting ready

As mentioned earlier in this chapter, it's always a good idea to think about the design of your new Dashboard before you dive headfirst into creating it. Once you're armed with that information you're ready to begin changing the basic structure of your new Dashboard.

How to do it...

1. Click the Dashboard icon on the navigation bar to access the Dashboard view.
2. Select the name of the new Dashboard that you want to modify from the **Dashboard** drop-down list and then click the **Edit Current Dashboard button** on the Dashboard tool bar. The Dashboard Designer opens.

3. Choose from any or all of the following options:
   - To *add* a new component right-click on a component, select **Insert** from the contextual menu and choose from one of the three options. As you can see in the following screenshot, you can add a new column, row, or even a new cell to the end of a row:

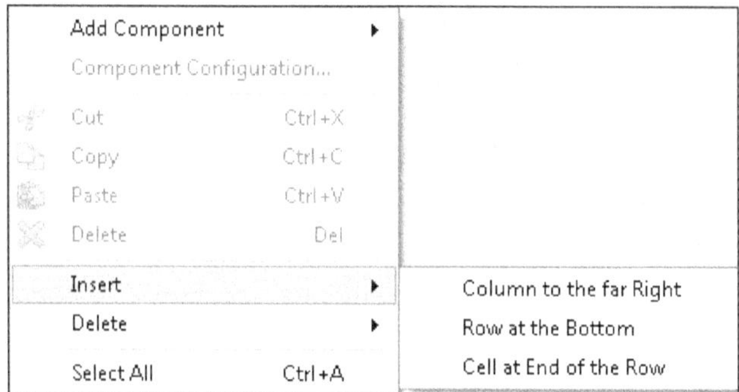

   - To delete a row or column right-click on a component, select **Delete** from the contextual menu and choose from one of the three options. You can delete a row or a column.
4. Click **File** and then choose **Exit** from the Dashboard Designer's menu bar to close the **Dashboard Designer**.
5. Click **Yes** to the dialog box to save your changes to the Dashboard.
6. Click **Close** to close the Dashboard Designer and then **Yes** to save the changes to the Dashboard.

How it works...

You may be a bit disappointed when you look at your newly customized Dashboard in the Dashboard view because it will be entirely blank and you won't be able to see the fruits of your labor. Not to worry; once you start adding data components to the cells of your Dashboard your masterpiece will become visible.

There's more...

Don't spend too much time worrying about the exact location when adding or removing rows or columns to your new Dashboard. After all, the entire Dashboard is virtually blank. The important thing here is to identify how many components you want to have in your final Dashboards and knowing if you're going to arrange them in rows or columns.

Creating wider components

By default, ACT! provides you with six identical-sized cells when you create a new Dashboard. However, you can also create a *double-wide* component if the need arises. For example, you may decide that one of the components in your brand new Dashboard is going to use the list view format, and that you would like to include numerous columns in that component. Using the default component sizing conventions means that you'll probably have to use the horizontal scroll bars to see all of the columns like in the following screenshot:

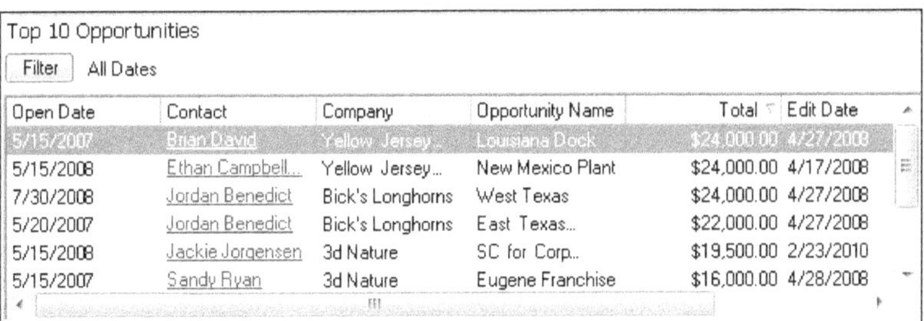

Getting ready

If you think you're going to be creating a list component on your Dashboard you may want to think about which fields you'll want to have display on the component. For example, if you're creating a component based on opportunity information you may give some thought to the opportunity fields you want to include.

How to do it...

1. Click the Dashboard icon on the navigation bar to access the Dashboard view.
2. Select the name of the new Dashboard that you want to modify from the **Dashboard** drop-down list and then click the **Edit Current Dashboard button** on the Dashboard tool bar. The **Dashboard Designer** opens.
3. Right-click on the row where you'd like to include the component, chose **Delete**, and then select **Cell at End of the Row** from the contextual menu. You'll notice that the component on the left will now expand to fill the space formerly used by the deleted component.
4. Click **File** and then choose **Save** from the Dashboard Designer's menu bar to save your changes.
5. Click **File** and then choose **Exit** from the Dashboard Designer's menu bar to close the **Dashboard Designer**.

How it works...

Unfortunately, if you think something magical will happen when you return to the Dashboard view you may be a bit disappointed. You won't be able to see the results of your work until you add additional component information to the cell.

Adding components to the Dashboard

Once you've created the framework for your Dashboard the sky's the limit, at least when it comes to adding ACT! components. You can easily mix and match the various Dashboard Components to create the ultimate Dashboard.

Getting ready

You may want to take a trip over to *Chapter 7, Working with the ACT! Dashboards* of this book if you don't feel entirely comfortable with the various components included in ACT!. It's always a good idea to determine the components that will best work for you prior to heading for the Dashboard Designer.

How to do it...

1. Click the Dashboard icon on the navigation bar to access the Dashboard view.
2. Select the name of the new Dashboard from the **Dashboard** drop-down list and then click the **Edit Current Dashboard button** on the Dashboard tool bar. The Dashboard Designer opens.
3. Click the cell that will contain the new Component to select it.
4. Click **Tools** from the Dashboard Designer toolbar, choose **Add Component**, select **Activities** or **Opportunities**, and then select the name of the component that you'd like to add. The **Component Configuration** wizard for the component you just selected will open. The following screenshot gives you an idea of what those menu items look like:

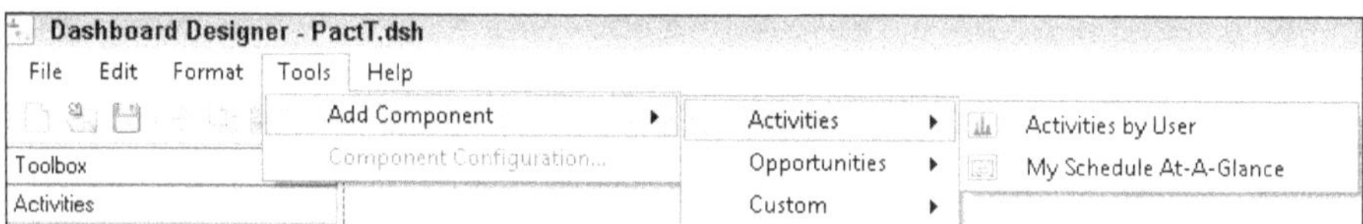

5. Make the appropriate changes to the new component.
6. Click **Close** to close the configuration Wizard.
7. Repeat steps 3 through 6 above to add additional components to the Dashboard.

8. Click **File** and then choose **Save** from the Dashboard Designer's menu bar to save your changes.
9. Click **File** and then choose **Exit** from the Dashboard Designer's menu bar to close the **Dashboard Designer**.

How it works...

Your new Dashboard will now reflect the addition of the various components that you just added.

There's more...

Don't worry if you have to create lots of similar Dashboards. Remember that once you create a new Dashboard, it's easy to clone it by simply saving it as a different name. For example, you may want to create a series of Opportunities Dashboard based on different Record Managers, or Activity Dashboards using different date filters.

Editing the new component

If you're not sure how to edit the new component and make it your own, you may want to take a peek at *Chapter 8, Filtering Dashboards* and *Chapter 9, Editing Existing Dashboards* of this book where you can get a refresher on editing a Dashboard Component. Remember, you can return to the Component Configuration wizard as often as you need to make sure that your component is displaying exactly the information you want.

Adding additional components to the new Dashboard

By default, new Dashboards contain enough empty cells to include six components. Once you've used up all the available cells you'll have to either create a few more cells or create another new Dashboard.

Adding data charts to the Dashboard

Adding new data chart components to a Dashboard follows almost the same exact steps as adding a regular component. The only difference is that you won't work with the Component Configuration wizard and you won't have the same number of options from which to choose.

You can **mix and match** data charts and components on your Dashboard to give you the exact information you are looking for.

Getting ready

As of this writing the dozen data charts that come with ACT! include the following:

- Recently created contacts
- Recently edited contacts
- Contact history count by history type
- Contacts by country
- Contacts by department
- Opportunities open by product
- Opportunities with contact info
- Opportunities by products
- Opportunity weighted total by stage
- Remote database information by user
- Remote database sync status by user
- User status

It's a good idea to be familiar with the available data charts so that you'll have a good idea of how to organize them before you head to the Dashboard Designer.

How to do it...

1. Click the Dashboard icon on the navigation bar to access the Dashboard view.
2. Select the name of the new Dashboard from the **Dashboard** drop-down list and then click the **Edit Current Dashboard button** on the Dashboard tool bar. The **Dashboard Designer** opens.
3. Click the cell that will contain the new data chart to select it.
4. Click **Tools** from the **Dashboard Designer** toolbar, choose **Add Component**, select **Custom**, and then select **Data Chart**. The **Data Chart Designer** will appear on the scene and the **Contact History Count by History Type** data chart will appear on your Dashboard.
5. Select the name of the data chart you want to add to your Dashboard from the **Choose a Template** drop-down list.
6. Customize the data chart by filing in any of the available fields.
7. Repeat steps 3 through 6 above to add additional data charts to the Dashboard.
8. Click **File** and then choose **Save** from the Dashboard Designer's menu bar to save your changes.
9. Click **File** and then choose **Exit** from the Dashboard Designer's menu bar to close the **Dashboard Designer**.

How it works...

Your newly selected data chart will now appear on your Dashboard displaying the appropriate information.

There's more...

As of this writing, there were a dozen data charts from which to choose. Hopefully that number will expand over time and will be included with future update patches and hot fixes. And, because it's so easy for third-party vendors to produce new data charts, you may also be able to purchase some in the very near future.

Customizing your data chart

The options available to you will vary according to the data chart you select. For example, the Opportunity Weighted Total by Stage data chart allows you to specify a chart type, add legends and labels, and supply both a header and a footer. However, many of the other data charts will only allow you to add a header and a footer.

Changing the order of the Dashboard components

One of the things you'll learn to love about ACT! is its flexibility. No matter how much forethought you put into the design of your new Dashboard you'll probably want to tweak it slightly to get it just right. Of course, you can always head back to the previous Dashboard chapters of this book if you need a bit of a refresher in editing your Dashboard but there is one last trick up the sleeve, namely, the ability to easily change the position of the Dashboard components.

There is no *right or wrong* way to arrange the various Dashboard Components. Some of you may like to have all the charts and graphs together in one area, and the lists in another. Others of you may prefer to jazz up the boring list by sprinkling in the more colorful charts. The bottom line is if you don't like the overall design you can literally drag any of the components to a new location.

Getting ready

Take a good look at your Dashboard to decide if it is artistically pleasing—or at the very least easy to understand.

How to do it...

1. Click the Dashboard icon on the navigation bar to access the Dashboard view.
2. Select the name of the new Dashboard from the **Dashboard** drop-down list and then click the **Edit Current Dashboard button** on the Dashboard tool bar. The **Dashboard Designer** opens.
3. Maximize the Dashboard Designer window if it is not already maximized.
4. Drag a component to the new location on the Dashboard.
5. Continue dragging the components around the Dashboard until you are pleased with the results.
6. Click **File** and then choose **Save** from the Dashboard Designer's menu bar to save your changes.
7. Click **File** and then choose **Exit** from the Dashboard Designer's menu bar to close the **Dashboard Designer**.

How it works...

The various components will now appear in their new locations.

There's more...

If you drag a component to a **double-wide** space it will automatically resize and expand to fill the larger area. Alternatively, if you drag a *double-wide* component to a smaller space it will automatically resize and contract to fit the smaller space.

Making horizontal moves

If you want to swap the order of components in the same row simple drag a component directly over the component to its right or left, depending on where you want the component to appear. The existing component will move out of the way. Unfortunately however, this will not work if you want to rearrange the order in a column of components; you can only move components vertically into an empty cell.

Index

Symbols

A

B

C

D

P

Q

R

S

T

W

X

Z

Thank you for buying
Sage ACT! 2011 Dashboard and Report Cookbook

About Packt Publishing

Packt, pronounced 'packed', published its first book "*Mastering phpMyAdmin for Effective MySQL Management*" in April 2004 and subsequently continued to specialize in publishing highly focused books on specific technologies and solutions.

Our books and publications share the experiences of your fellow IT professionals in adapting and customizing today's systems, applications, and frameworks. Our solution-based books give you the knowledge and power to customize the software and technologies you're using to get the job done. Packt books are more specific and less general than the IT books you have seen in the past. Our unique business model allows us to bring you more focused information, giving you more of what you need to know, and less of what you don't.

Packt is a modern, yet unique publishing company, which focuses on producing quality, cutting-edge books for communities of developers, administrators, and newbies alike. For more information, please visit our website: `www.PacktPub.com`.

About Packt Enterprise

In 2010, Packt launched two new brands, Packt Enterprise and Packt Open Source, in order to continue its focus on specialization. This book is part of the Packt Enterprise brand, home to books published on enterprise software - software created by major vendors, including (but not limited to) IBM, Microsoft and Oracle, often for use in other corporations. Its titles will offer information relevant to a range of users of this software, including administrators, developers, architects, and end users.

Writing for Packt

We welcome all inquiries from people who are interested in authoring. Book proposals should be sent to `author@packtpub.com`. If your book idea is still at an early stage and you would like to discuss it first before writing a formal book proposal, contact us; one of our commissioning editors will get in touch with you.

We're not just looking for published authors; if you have strong technical skills but no writing experience, our experienced editors can help you develop a writing career, or simply get some additional reward for your expertise.

www.ingramcontent.com/pod-product-compliance
Lightning Source LLC
LaVergne TN
LVHW062315060326
832902LV00013B/2229

* 9 7 8 1 8 4 9 6 8 1 9 2 6 *